HEART CALLS,
SOUL ANSWERS

HEART CALLS,
SOUL ANSWERS
~ *What Do You Want Me to Learn Today?* ~

BIRAJ WAYNE PALMER

Blue Bones Books
Santa Cruz, CA 95063

Copyright © 2019 by Biraj Wayne Palmer
All rights reserved. Published 2019.
First edition.

Printed in U.S.A.
1 3 5 7 9 10 8 6 4 2

ISBN-13:
978-1-948675-02-4

EBOOK WITHOUT PAGE NUMBERS:
978-1-948675-03-1

LIBRARY OF CONGRESS
201-99-10916

Edited by Rambhakta Beinhorn

Cover and interior designed by
Tejindra Scott Tully

☙ Blue Bone Books ❧
www.bluebonebooks.com

In Gratitude to:

My guru Paramhansa Yogananda,
my spiritual teachers Swami Kriyananda,
Nayaswamis Jyotish and Devi,
Asha Nayaswami, Shanti Rubenstone,
Nayaswami Dharmadas, Vidura Smallen,
Narayani Anaya, and my very first
spiritual teacher, Naomi Palmer.

*Special thanks for help in
the making of this book to:*

JLove Jackson, Nayaswami Lakshman,
Mahavir Hernandez, Nayaswami Nishkama,
Nayaswami Rambhakta, Rammurti and Sita Reed,
Robin Lysne, Susan Hoffert, Tejindra Tully,
and most of all, the woman who keeps
challenging me to think of, and to love,
God and Guru more deeply every day of
my life, my wife Nayaswami Lahari.

Poem of Dedication
WHISPERS FROM ETERNITY
From the book of the same title, by Paramhansa Yogananda, edited by his direct disciple, Swami Kriyananda

I WAS DEAF, but Eternity whispered to me unceasingly. My wisdom's hearing-power slowly woke, and I heard the Whispers of Eternity becoming ever clearer in response to my sacred demands.

I asked Eternity: "What do Thy whispers mean?" The whispers grew stronger, until at last, quite suddenly, Eternity answered: "Hear the voice of uninterrupted guidance. I am God's spokesman, Eternity. I have whispered to thee through thy slumber of ages: 'Awake!' Now thou art awake, and My whispers will never cease from saying: 'Wake all thy brothers!' In sleeping minds everywhere, My whispers constantly work. Work thou with Me, through living, eternal whispers, that all may hear His voice."

I replied to Eternity: "I will send whispers to all my sleeping brothers, saying: 'Awake! Get ready! Come home to His perennial peace!' And I will borrow Thy voice, Eternity, when my earthly voice can be no more heard. Then I will continue to utter through Thee: "Oh, listen to His all-solacing soul-whispers!"

I will wait for all, uttering to them Eternity's whispers. As my countless human brothers—and also beasts, and atom-sparks—all slowly travel toward their own final freedom, their long train seemingly endless, I will softly say through these *Whispers from Eternity*: "Awake! Let us all together go home, following the whispered summons of His ever-calling voice."

CONTENTS

*Poem of Dedication:
from* Whispers from Eternity,
by Paramhansa Yogananda | v

Foreword: by Asha Nayaswami | ix

Preface: from The Imitation of Christ,
by Thomas à Kempis | xi

Introduction | xiii

Guide to Readers | xix

1. RIGHT ATTITUDE | 3

2. LEADERSHIP | 23

3. THE EFFORT TO FOCUS | 47

4. OVERCOMING THE EGO | 83

5. LOVE, DEVOTION, AND SURRENDER | 109

6. GOD IS THE DOER | 139

7. INTUITION OF GOD'S WILL | 165

8. PRESENCE OF GOD | 197

Afterword | 223

Glossary | 225

Bibliography | 231

Author Bio | 233

FOREWORD

by Asha Nayaswami

This is a book to be savored, not gulped.

It is a unique combination of established wisdom from saints and sages of many traditions, both ancient and modern, and insights from "Divine Mother"—God as the Comforter—as She speaks to the author, before, during, and sometimes after his daily meditation.

Biraj Palmer himself makes no special claims to insight. His life pattern is recognizably the same as most of his readers. A variety of jobs, starting with a dozen years as a preschool teacher, a stint in the publishing business, on staff at a well-known meditation retreat, years in India, then back to California to teach meditation at an urban center.

The consistent thread through these many decades has been a daily meditation practice, notebook close at hand, writing down the inspirations received.

"Many days it was ordinary journaling," Biraj says. "But every so often, something — more accurately, Someone — would take over, giving me words and wisdom greater than I could ever create on my own."

Learning to discern among the many inner voices that clamor for our attention is one of the most important, and most difficult, arts that every person who sincerely seeks to be closer to God must master.

The Divine and the mundane compete for our attention. Desires, hopes, fears, regrets cloud our judgment. Gradually, though, if we persevere with sincere longing for Truth, God speaks in a Voice we learn to trust like no other.

This is a collection of that Voice speaking, first to Biraj, then through him, to all of us.

What joy awaits you in this inspired collection.

ASHA NAYASWAMI
author, *Swami Kriyananda, Lightbearer*
The Life and Legacy of a Disciple of Paramhansa Yogananda

PREFACE

The Imitation of Christ, written in the 1420s, is called by Wikipedia "the most widely read devotional work next to the Bible." In it, the Divine is quoted as sharing these intuitive thoughts with the author:

"My son," says our Lord... "Give heed to My words, for they enflame the heart and enlighten the understanding... Even when you have read and understood many puzzling things, it nevertheless behooves you to come to One who is the Beginning of all things, that is, God Himself; otherwise, your knowledge will avail you little.

"I am He who teaches a man wisdom and gives more understanding to humble persons than can be given by man's teaching. And he to whom I speak will soon become wise and will advance much in spirit, but pain and woe will be to those who seek only for curious learning, taking little heed of the way to serve God...

"I am He who ... illuminates and lifts up a humble soul, so that it can take and receive in short time the true reason of the wisdom of God more perfectly than another who studies ten years in the schools and lacks humility. I teach without sound of words, without diversity of opinions, without desire for honor, and without strife and arguments. I am He who teaches all the people . . . to seek and savor eternal things, to flee honors, to bear patiently all evil words, to put their trust wholly in Me, to desire nothing without Me, and above all things fervently to love Me."

THOMAS À KEMPIS
The Imitation of Christ, p. 165

INTRODUCTION

The book you are about to read is filled with answered prayers.

It all began as I looked up wistfully into the full moon from the middle of a wide-open field of dry grass.

I had never realized that there was "More" than my own little self—until that night of quiet despair, all alone in that big field, with the power and majesty of an autumn full moon glaring down on me. I felt, for the first time, that someone, something, actually cared that I was unhappy, unfulfilled, confused, and utterly alone. I had no idea what "It" was. I only know that on that evening, I began my spiritual search.

Sure, I had spent plenty of episodes in my youth looking for something to believe in. The good thing is that the home I was raised in had no kind of religious dogma for me to rebel against. The problem, though, was that there wasn't any religious training of any kind. We were Unitarians, after all! Social do-goodism seemed to be our family religion. I certainly never remember hearing the G-word. My parents said they wished they could believe, but just hadn't found God to be personally impactful in their daily lives. I guess that wasn't enough for me, because whenever I could, I tagged along with young friends as they attended catechism or Sunday school or church services. Mormons, Baptists, born-again Christians, Charismatics, Religious Scientists, Unity, even Sufis—I tried every church I could find.

Unfortunately, I also gained a nasty addiction before I turned 20. And like so many before me, by my own power alone, I could not shake it.

Then came the lonely night in the middle of that huge field of dry grass, and that moon, shining down on me—*into* me. Hard to describe, but I was sure that moon *knew* me. I felt both exposed, and cleansed, all at the same time. It seemed to know of my struggles, and yet it accepted me—even *loved* me—for who I was. You might ask, how can a craggy sphere have any effect on one human being 93 million miles away? I have no answer to that. All I know is, my life began to change. And that night marked the beginning.

I spent the next twelve years in various attempts to figure out what it was I'd experienced that night, and more importantly, what could I do to get more of it.

That search led me eventually to the great Indian guru, Paramhansa Yogananda, author of the spiritual classic, *Autobiography of a Yogi*. Yogananda himself had left his body in 1952, the same year of my birth. His direct disciple, Swami Kriyananda, though, had established an ashram for disciples of Yogananda in the Sierra Nevada foothills outside Nevada City, California. In 1981, I learned the meditation techniques taught by these kind souls, helped to facilitate a local group of meditators in the San Francisco Bay Area for a while, then in 1984 decided, with my wife, to take the plunge of moving full-time to the ashram. It is called Ananda Village. Kriyananda often referred to it as an "intentional spiritual community." There were 300 other high-minded and open-hearted souls—singles, married couples, and children—

living in remarkable harmony together where they worked, played, meditated, and worshipped all in the same tight-knit community. It felt like paradise to a spiritual searcher like me.

I lived for the next 16 years at the ashram outside Nevada City, California. We raised our teenaged son there through his high school years. I worked at jobs ranging from school teaching, cashiering in our two health food stores, carpentry, selling books for our publishing company, and leading weekends at the community's retreat center. Then in 1999, my wife and I began a period of service outside of the original ashram, at a number of Ananda's satellite communities around the world: Palo Alto, CA; Rhode Island; Sacramento; Delhi and Pune, India; and currently back in Palo Alto. Morning sadhana of exercises, chanting, and meditation, with the practices of Kriya Yoga that Yogananda taught, has been a daily part of my life during all those years.

During that very first week of residence at Ananda Village, I started writing brief entries in a simple blank journal. Each took no more than 5 minutes to complete. Sometimes I wrote it at the start of my spiritual practices, sometimes in the middle, less often at the end (following the advice of my spiritual director, Jyotish Novak). Over the next 35 years, I filled forty of those journals. The entries you are about to read are some from those journals. You will find them, within each chapter, in the chronological order that I wrote them. I have let the entries speak for themselves. Occasionally, you will encounter a word in Sanskrit, the ancient language of yogis from India like Yogananda. If you are unfamiliar with such terms, you will find them defined in the glossary at the back of the book.

Each of the entries in my journals always began the same: "Dear Divine Ma, WDYWMTLT?" The capital letters always meant the same thing. The combination of letters in my request simply means: What do You want me to learn today? In the earliest days of journaling, I used to get myself writing by asking four questions, of which this one was the last. But in time, I found that just this one simple question worked fine all by itself.

It wasn't always easy. There were times that complete nonsense came out onto the page—ego-filled statements that in time I realized were simply reflections of my own subconscious mind. At other times, statements of surprising wisdom popped out onto the page. At first, I couldn't easily tell the difference. In time, however, I began to realize that when the subconscious stuff came out, it felt one way, and when one of those moments of wisdom appeared, it felt quite different. It seemed to have a different "ring" or vibration to it. Later on, I came to call it less mental, more devotional—less from the mind, and more from the heart. And if I followed any advice from this latter type, it always worked out well. Tuning into that difference allowed me to stop giving energy when the subconscious stuff was trying to grab my attention. I learned to turn my back on that stream of consciousness, right in the middle of a sentence of thought. I learned from my own experience that that feeling wasn't going to lead to any entry that would prove useful. And then I would just wait until that "other voice" would fill the vacuum. In time, it always did. It's as if I had to physically "lift" my awareness out of the gutters of the subconscious, and hold it, uplifted, waiting, for that source of what Yogananda, Kriyananda, and others have often called "the superconscious."

This book is all about ways to conduct that journey for yourself. It's a veritable handbook, filled with scores of tools and attitudes from the wisest of spiritual teachers on how to safely and successfully access intuitive inner guidance from the superconscious. More personally, the book is filled with some of the results of one man's journey following those tools, and what I learned as a result. My hope is that these writings will show that everyone—anyone—has a chance to access that same connection. It's not just for saints, or special people lost to the dusty pages of history. Regular people have made that connection too. Lots of them have.

This book is filled with advice on how you, too, could do it. The greatest saints and sages down through the ages have always taught this to their close disciples. There is nothing secret, or mysterious, about intuition. Intuition is for everyone. It is our birthright. It is up to us to open up to this potential that is waiting within each of us.

Some people talk about accessing intuition. Others talk about communing with a power greater than one's self. That Power has been called by many names. Whether the seeker calls it God, Jesus, Jehovah, Allah, Abba, Ishwara, Bhagavan, the Buddha, Elohim, HaShem, Divine Mother, Superconsciousness, or Cosmic Ground of Being is less important. What is important is that we each, individually, put out the effort to connect with It, and to commune with It.

My own personal tools of choice for connecting with It have been Kriya Yoga and journaling. Each must find his or her own way. It has often been stated that truth is one; paths are many. Whatever path one chooses, all humans ultimately share the same goal: unending happiness, or Joy. In the West, seekers often say this comes through Mystical Marriage. In the East, seekers often say this comes from a Union with All That Is. That latter happens to be the underlying meaning of the word yoga, and, I believe, a useful shorthand for the ultimate goal of all spiritual practices.

Here is what my beloved spiritual teacher Swami Kriyananda has said about this possibility of connecting with All That Is:

> My own experience convinces me that the Divine *is* accessible to any of us. That's what the saints and sages of all religions have always been trying to communicate to us. Not that they were special, but that we all can be so blessed—if we completely let down our mental barriers. Don't let discouragement get the better of you. Don't give up. If you truly make a sincere, sustained effort to reach out and connect, the Divine wants to meet us half way. The Divine is only waiting for you to "open your heart to Me, and I will enter and take charge of your life."

My sincere wish is that you, too, find Her waiting for you.

BIRAJ PALMER
Palo Alto, California
July 4, 2019

GUIDE TO READERS

When you see a paragraph in the manuscript that has orange brackets around it, it had been clear to me that my own rational mind was thinking those thoughts. But if a particular paragraph is shown with quotation marks around it, that signifies a message that came from a Source wiser than my own conscious mind. I, in my egoic self, am not that smart. You are free to call that Source whatever feels best to you. I just know that when I follow It, it works.

You might wonder why I chose to address my daily requests to "Divine Mother." When Paramhansa Yogananda talked about God, he talked about "Mother." He wanted us to find a way to be intimate with God. "Master" told us that the mother was closer than the father—less severe, more accepting.

The stern disciplinarian of the Old Testament had no appeal for me. Even the "God as father" that Jesus addressed seemed a bit aloof. Master and Swamiji's "Divine Mother" felt approachable, forgiving, understanding, and totally accepting. I could be drawn to this aspect of divinity. Intellectually, I realized that God had to be bigger than any private image I held of Her. But God of the entire universe seemed too big for me to handle, so this thought of Divine Mother was something to which I could relate. With this, I felt completely loved, no fear of judgment, even confident. I could open my heart to such a God—open my very soul. So, in 1984, I began writing questions to "Dear Divine Ma."

In a somewhat related vein, for the poem "Whispers from Eternity" that begins this book, some people today would prefer that Yogananda had used the word "friend" in lieu of "brother," to be inclusive of both women and men. Yogananda wrote down this statement in the 1930's, which was a time quite different from ours, with different mores. But more to the point, Yogananda tells us that poems like this one were not even composed by him, but rather *received* from a Source beyond. He was simply the scribe. The editors chose not to change Yogananda's language in any way. That way readers could hear the Master's original wording, but be able to make a mental translation themselves if they felt the need.

Nevertheless, whenever the one I chose to call Divine Mother communicated with me, She most often used the terms "He" or "Him" when referring to God. I merely and humbly report this as a simple observation.

HEART CALLS,
SOUL ANSWERS
~ *What Do You Want Me to Learn Today?* ~

CHAPTER 1

RIGHT ATTITUDE

Intuition can be developed—not by all, perhaps, but by many people—with practice. There is a certain feeling that comes when true intuition is at work, as opposed to the mere enthusiasms of imagination.

~ Swami Kriyananda ~
The Art of Supportive Leadership, p. 65

LIFE IS TO BE ENJOYED, BUT NOT DEPENDED UPON

*Dear Divine Ma,
What do You want me to learn today?*

"Depend on God, not people or things.
Enjoy everything that comes to you as a gift
from God—the joys as well as the sorrows.
As Yogananda said, this world is meant
for our entertainment and our education.
Don't expect the events of your life to give you
more than that. Be content, whatever comes—
accept it as coming from God's hands.
Where else would it come from?
God is all there is—and God is love, therefore
love is all there is. And if this is so, then
you, too, are unconditionally, eternally loved.
There is nothing to fear.
'Love *is* letting go of fear.'"*

~ AUGUST 2004 ~

* Gerald Jampolsky, *Love Is Letting Go of Fear*

YOUR REACTIVITY DETERMINES WHETHER YOU ARE HAPPY

*Dear Divine Ma,
What do You want me to learn today?*

"'Remain unshaken amidst the crash of breaking worlds.'* 'Be in your spine,'† no matter what. Never let people know that they have ruffled you. If they could see what you know to be true, they could also stay calm. But until you realize that you and your Heavenly Father are one, there will be little chance of your remaining calmly centered when troubles break around you. Remember that your happiness depends not on what goes on in the world around you, but what is happening in your consciousness. It's your reactivity that determines whether you'll be happy or not. Be blessed by all things. Resist nothing. 'What comes of itself, let it come.'"‡

~ SEPTEMBER 2004 ~

* Ancient Indian saying
† Paramhansa Yogananda, *How to Be Happy All the Time*, p. 128
‡ Paramhansa Yogananda

*Intuition is that
faculty of the soul [that]
at once directly perceives
the truth about anything.
Without the power of intuition,
you cannot know Truth.
Intuition means "soul-perception,"
and is the knowing power
of the soul, without the help
of the senses or the mind.
Intuition can give you
knowledge about things
that your senses and understanding can never give.*

~ **Paramhansa Yogananda** ~
How to Have Courage, Calmness, and Confidence, p. 117

DON'T STRIVE–BE!

*Dear Divine Ma,
What do You want me to learn today?*

{ What is it that "D" wanted me to learn about working with servants in India? As Swami put it, "More dignity would become you nicely." It would be good to cultivate a certain reserve in your dealings with others. Be kind and gentle, but dignified and somewhat reserved. Yes, like J—— always living centered in the spine. Never fawning over others. Never trying to be liked. Just being himself. Just doing what's appropriate. }*

"Those who are dedicated to serving this work have a definite role to play in this life, and it's not about making friends with everyone. It is entirely a question of sharing God's light. You must live in that light before you can offer it to others. And if you're grasping for anything at all, including the desire to be thought fair and kind and nice, you won't be able to stay in the light. Don't strive. Just be."

~ OCTOBER 2004 ~

---

* My voice (as opposed to Ma's) will be differentiated by these colored brackets.

FIND YOUR HAPPINESS WITHIN

*Dear Divine Ma,
What do You want me to learn today?*

"Can a mere change of circumstances make you truly happy? No. Happiness is an 'inside job.' You must make yourself happy—or, more to the point, you must find happiness *within*. No one can escape this truth. No mere *thing* can give you happiness. No *place* can make you happy if you aren't deeply determined already to be happy. 'If you choose to be unhappy, no one can make you happy.'* Happiness is a state of mind. We bless the world by our uplifted consciousness, and we pull the world down when we choose to cling to lower states. Do what's needed for the uplifted consciousness that God wants to give you."

~ DECEMBER 2005 ~

*Paramhansa Yogananda

Don't jump up the moment you've done your [meditation practices]. Sit still awhile; enjoy the inner peace. That is how intuition *is developed: Prolong and deepen as much as possible the peaceful aftereffects of practicing the techniques.*

~ Swami Kriyananda ~
Conversations with Yogananda, #390

YOUR OWN INNER CONTENTMENT

*Dear Divine Ma,
What do You want me to learn today?*

"Learn moderation in all things.
If you don't get what you want, you pout and hold a grudge until you get it.
Or you try to get it by your own power.
Why do you keep looking outside your Self for that which will make you happy?
Haven't you learned that nothing outside of the higher Self can last?

"Your inner contentment is the only happiness you take with you wherever you go.
All else will fail you. *All!!!* Find joy now.
It is the only thing you can count on.
'Be thou therefore a yogi.'* Turn within.
All else is delusion. 'Get away from My ocean of suffering.'† Find Him now."

~ OCTOBER 2007 ~

---

* Bhagavan Krishna in the Bhagavad Gita   † ibid.

WITH RIGHT ATTITUDE, YOU HAVE EVERYTHING

*Dear Divine Ma,
What do You want me to learn today?*

"It isn't where you live, but *how* you live that matters.
You can live in a city and be a beast.
You can live in the countryside and be a beast.
Or you can live in the countryside and be
innocent and pure. Or you can live in the city and be
innocent and pure. It's not a question of wealth,
or locale, or luxuries, or even simplicity.
It's all about consciousness.

"You can live in a castle and be depraved, and you
can live in a mud hut and be king of your domain.
Which consciousness do you choose?

"It all depends on your choices, your actions,
and even more, your attitudes. If you have
the right attitude, you have everything.
If you have the wrong attitude, though you
own millions, you are lost."

~ SEPTEMBER 2008 ~

If you hold onto the calmness that comes after meditation, then you will be guided aright. Intuition guides your reason. When you have developed intuition, you will stand firm in your knowledge, though the universe rise up to defeat you.

Whenever you want to solve a problem intuitively, first go into deep meditation or silence. Do not think of your problem during meditation, but meditate until you feel a sense of calmness filling the inner recesses of your body, and your breath becomes calm and quiet.

Then ask God to direct your intuition so that you know what you should do.

~ **Paramhansa Yogananda** ~
How to Have Courage, Calmness, and Confidence, p. 118

CONTROL YOUR PEACE OF MIND

*Dear Divine Ma,
What do You want me to learn today?*

"It's time to truly take charge of the project. Do your *dharma*. Get the things in place that the project needs. And then just stand firm— not narrowly insistent, but unruffled in the confidence about what simply *is*. Your role is to do the best you can, given the tools available. Get what you need, but remain unruffled. Your peace of mind is something that you can control. Very little else will actually be under your control. Accept what is, and flow with it gracefully. Be full of grace, and then you won't feel such a need to give people 'a piece of your mind.'"

~ MAY 2009 ~

DHARMA AS YOUR SOURCE

*Dear Divine Ma,
What do You want me to learn today?*

"It's time to learn patience. You need to allow time for the fruits of your new spiritual efforts, your new *tapasya*, to manifest. They won't appear overnight! They are tender shoots that need to be nurtured and protected. The best gardener knows that it's only by opening his heart to the tender seedlings that they that will produce bountifully. Love these good new traits in yourself and they will blossom spectacularly.

"In the meantime, keep the weeds of evil thoughts rigorously and devotedly at bay. Do your daily round of weeding and introspecting. 'How did they on the battlefield?' Which side is winning, the Kauravas or the Pandavas* in your life? The Kauravas have so many soldiers clamoring for victory, while the Pandavas have just a few. But those few are infused with righteous power—with *dharma*—as their source, and only Good."

~ JULY 2009 ~

* Bhagavad Gita

The best way ... intuition [can] be developed is, every time you meditate, to sit calmly for a long time after doing the techniques. It is during this period that you will be able to deepen your awareness of God's presence within you.

Go ever deeper in your enjoyment of that presence. The longer and more deeply you enjoy the peace within, the more quickly will your intuition develop.

~ **Paramhansa Yogananda** ~
The Essence of Self-Realization, p. 173

CHOOSE UPLIFTMENT EVERY DAY

*Dear Divine Ma,
What do You want me to learn today?*

"Can you learn to love as A—— loves, completely without judgment or expectation? It's easy to find fault with people and situations; it's much more difficult to say only positive things. When J—— made the effort never to speak ill of others, it was a true, and very deep spiritual practice. It's wonderful to discipline our consciousness to remain always expansive in this way.

"If you want to think only the best of others, you must first learn to speak only the best of them. Our negative thoughts create a downward-pulling energy that others can feel. Positive thoughts generate an energy that can uplift them. Which kind of energy do you want to generate? Would you welcome a daily diet of negative energy?

"Of course not! Yet isn't that what you're choosing, when you complain about others? Choose uplifting thoughts, speech, and actions throughout each day. Think of the difference it will make in your life. Imagine the possibilities!"

~ JULY 2011 ~

THE CONSCIOUSNESS WITH WHICH WE HAVE DONE IT

*Dear Divine Ma,
What do You want me to learn today?*

{ We are having a wonderful time helping You as You create our little community for Ananda. Certainly there have been disappointments and petty disagreements. But, wow, what a job this has been! Where else could I have had a chance to do so much for You and Swamiji? I'm saddened that I'm not sure Swamiji is particularly pleased with what I've done. Of course, the only thing he cares about is not what we accomplish, but the quality of the consciousness we build through our service. And that is the key, isn't it? It doesn't matter a whit what we've done, only the consciousness with which we've done it. That's the only structure that Swamiji is interested in building—the edifice of our consciousness. And whatever the result, if attained with lightness of consciousness, Swamiji would welcome it. But if done with a heavy, negative, or berating consciousness—without *dharma* as our guide— any result, regardless how grand, would most certainly meet with his indifference. }

~ JANUARY 2012 ~

*You must be solution-oriented
to draw guidance, and you
must have the courage to ask.
Try to free your mind from
the static of doubt, and strongly
hold the thought, "There is
an answer, and it will come to me
if I seek in the right way."*

~ **Swami Kriyananda** ~
Intuition for Starters, p. 35

DROP THE ACT, AND BE WHO YOU REALLY ARE

*Dear Divine Ma,
What do You want me to learn today?*

{ Hello there. It's been awhile. Where in the world do I go when I turn my consciousness away from You? I reckon I've forgotten You while wandering in *maya*'s thrall. The world pulls me away over and over again. }

"You are precious to Me. You allow yourself to become lost in the things of this world, as you say, over and over. Paramhansa Yogananda lamented how the desire for name and fame takes the disciples away. For you, it's fortunately a lesser allure, of wanting to be known as someone who can accomplish things, though you can too easily slip into wanting to do only what you want. What you wish people to think about you, and how you actually want to act, are no longer in harmony. There would be less tension if you would drop the act, and simply be who you really are."

~ AUGUST 2013 ~

CRITICS ARE YOUR BEST FRIENDS

*Dear Divine Ma,
What do You want me to learn today?*

"Don't take others' criticism so personally. Critics are there to help you grow. They are your best friends, because they won't let you get away with behaviors about which others don't care enough to scold you. Critics are God helping you become aware of your faults, so that you can get busy and change them. 'Let me therefore face my faults with gratitude,' as the affirmation says, 'for only by facing them can I work on them, and change them.'* Without critics, how will you learn what needs improving?"

~ JUNE 2015 ~

* Swami Kriyananda, *Affirmations for Self-Healing*

CHAPTER 2

LEADERSHIP

> People often struggle for a long time to find the *guidance* they want. No time is really needed: only sufficient mental clarity and energy.
>
> ~ **Swami Kriyananda** ~
> *Intuition for Starters*, p. 35

LOVE MORE, JUDGE LESS

*Dear Divine Ma,
What do You want me to learn today?*

"I want you to be vigilant in disciplining *yourself*, and always forgiving in how you treat *others*. Exercise judgment and discrimination only toward yourself, correcting your faults and weaknesses, never those of others. Judging others is never warranted. Always let God be the judge—your job is to love; that is all. Love is the *only* commodity in this world that is forever in short supply. Love more, and judge less. Let the world discover the joy of meditation by how much you love. That is a secret worth sharing."

~ JULY 2004 ~

BE KIND

*Dear Divine Ma,
What do You want me to learn today?*

"It's time you learned how to share what you know with others in ways that don't alienate them. An excellent mantra for you is, 'Be kind.' You've done a marvelous job of pushing many projects through to completion. And now it's time to shift gears. This new job will be harder for you. You must learn to be a supportive leader, no longer a 'bulldozer.' Reread Swamiji's book on leadership. Watch his leadership video. And *learn*. You must learn not to react. You won't have the luxury now of being easily knocked off your center. You must think of the welfare of others. 'People *are* more important than things!'"*

~ SEPTEMBER 2004 ~

* Swami Kriyananda, *The Art of Supportive Leadership*

*The more you seek to be
guided by intuition, which is
an aspect of superconsciousness,
the greater success you will
meet in every undertaking.
For the rational mind can only
point to probable solutions.
Intuition, rooted as it is in
superconsciousness, will supply
you with clear answers.*

~ Swami Kriyananda ~
Awaken to Superconsciousness, p. 243

BE A BEACON OF LIGHT

*Dear Divine Ma,
What do You want me to learn today?*

"Just keep your heart open.
It isn't terribly important *what* you do,
but only *how* you do it.
Bless others by your presence.
If you judge those with whom you work,
your attitude will poison your ability to love.
Help others by giving them your love and respect.
Bless those with whom you work,
not only those whom you are asked to serve.
Your job is to be a beacon of light,
shining not only outward to the world,
but also inward to your own team."

~ NOVEMBER 2004 ~

WORK WITH PEOPLE

*Dear Divine Ma,
What do You want me to learn today?*

"You are working too hard. When you serve Me, do so with your consciousness centered calmly in the spine. If you work centered in your spine, and if you make good use of the people around you, you'll be able to do twice as much in half the time. You must 'learn to work *with* people.'* Remember that it isn't a question of how *hard* you work, but of how *smart* you work. That is the greatest key to success. We all love you, but people sometimes can't stand to be around you. Why?

"You don't take others' realities into account. When you are judgmental, it repels the people you need to work *with*. When you try to get work 'out of' others, they feel it. It's very off-putting! Bless them—never criticize. They, too, are working *toward* their own eventual sainthood— why would you expect them to be perfect already? You are quite aware of your own faults; why not be compassionate for the faults they're probably just as aware of in themselves? Bring out the best in people, not the worst, by focusing all of your attention on the good in them."

~ APRIL 2005 ~

* Swami Kriyananda, *The Art of Supportive Leadership*

With a degree of tentative self-offering, rely more and more on the guidance that you feel from within. You will find that in little ways, and then in big ways, you will be guided. This loving guidance will be with you in amazing ways, and constantly.

~ Swami Kriyananda ~
A Handbook on Discipleship, p. 54

QUIET DOES MORE GOOD THAN RAVING

*Dear Divine Ma,
What do You want me to learn today?*

"Learn to be humble. Recognize that you don't know everything, and that others might be able to do things that you couldn't do. Accepting their help graciously would be a major victory for you, and for Ananda. You are proud and tough, but do those qualities reflect well on the organization? Be at peace. Be respectful. Be in good humor. Not just when people do what you want, but when they don't. Be at peace! Your quiet will do more good than any amount of reactive shouting will ever do."

~ JUNE 2009 ~

LIVE IN JOY, BUT EXPECT NOTHING FROM ANYONE

Dear Divine Ma,
What do You want me to learn today?

"Expect nothing from others. They have their own expectations and needs. If you impose your own goals on them, you'll only end up clashing with them. Expect nothing. Be attached to nothing. Desire is the source of all suffering. Feel the simple blessing of being alive. Live in Joy. But expect nothing from anyone. That is the way to unending bliss. This is the way to live in harmony with everybody. 'Wrath springs only from thwarted desires. I do not expect anything from others, so their actions can not be in opposition to wishes of mine.'* 'Desire is the cause of all suffering.'" †

~ JULY 2009 ~

---

* Swami Sri Yukteswar, in *Autobiography of a Yogi*
† Gautama Buddha

Paramhansa Yogananda gave a powerful affirmation to help us develop the courage to act on our inner guidance.
"I will reason, I will will, and I will act, but guide [Thou] my reason, will, and activity to the right path in everything."

Drawing intuitive guidance is a cooperative effort. We must be willing to act, but with the realization that a higher consciousness is working with us and guiding our efforts.

~ Swami Kriyananda ~
Intuition for Starters, p. 65

LET OTHERS BE PART OF THE TEAM

*Dear Divine Ma,
What do You want me to learn today?*

{ Divine Mother, there's a trend that I'm noticing recently in Your responses. It seems that I must make a change. Less pushing; more magnetizing. }

"Inspire others, and they will *want* to work for you. Get them laughing and enjoying the vision of the goal. A supportive leader helps those in his charge to understand *why* they are doing the work, not just the *how* of it. This approach will inspire them. Keep in mind the greater vision of what's being done, and learn to communicate it to others. It will help them more clearly understand 'what's trying to happen.'*
Feel that the workers are your partners in creating something unique and special. Otherwise, it will seem like drudgery to them. Let them feel valued and important as part of the team. Their contributions *are* invaluable. If you serve in that spirit, each day will bring you into closer alignment with My will."

~ MAY 2009 ~

* Steven Gaskin, quoted by Swami Kriyananda

COMPLETED PROJECTS, OR VIBRATIONS OF LOVE?

*Dear Divine Ma,
What do You want me to learn today?*

"What you are looking for is a transformation of consciousness. Why would God want anything else for you but to lift you into a higher level of awareness? His sole desire is to transform you into one of His saints. And, in order to cooperate with His plan for you, it's crucial that you cultivate harmony of mind. If you lose your peace, what can you offer to the world that will be of any lasting value? Is anything else worth offering?

"What legacy do you want to leave to the planet: a wake of projects completed, or a swath of people who feel loved? It's your choice. What is it that will help the world in a lasting way—completed projects, or vibrations of love? Learn to love. For those who don't want to work with you, just bless them and move on. Get the job done, without judging others. Remember, 'They are *all* My children.'* Give them My love." †

~ JUNE 2009 ~

* Babaji to Swami Kriyananda, in Asha Nayaswami's *Lightbearer*
† Swami Kriyananda, in the movie *Finding Happiness*

Intuition is soul guidance, appearing naturally in man during those instants when his mind is calm. Nearly everyone has had the experience of an inexplicably correct "hunch."

~ **Paramhansa Yogananda** ~
Autobiography of a Yogi, p. 153

I AM IN ERROR WHEN I SEE AUGHT BUT YOU, MA

*Dear Divine Ma,
What do You want me to learn today?*

"There is only one thing worth doing, and that is to find God. All else is diversion and distraction. Bless everyone who abuses you, for they too are a part of God. God is in every one of us. Where is there that God is not? Why judge or condemn anybody for what they do? They are all children of God. Whether pure or lesser channels of divinity is the only question."

{ Dear Lord, help me to judge no one. Help me to see only Thee shining forth from the eyes of even your erring children, my divine brothers and sisters. Bless me that I see only You wherever I look, dearest Ma. I am the one in error when I see aught but You—everywhere, all-pervading. I have been blind. }

~ JULY 2009 ~

EXPERIENCE A THING WITHOUT JUDGING IT

*Dear Divine Ma,
What do You want me to learn today?*

"Practice non-judgment. Too often you divide the experience of life's wholeness into tidy boxes of 'I like' and 'I don't like.' Aren't there categories that are more important? Wouldn't it work out better for you if you would simply experience without judging, criticizing, condemning, critiquing, pigeon-holing, categorizing, naming, or cutting others down? These actions belittle your experience; they shrink it down smaller than its potential.

"Why not simply experience your life in its essential purity and simplicity? In every experience there are many nuances that you will either miss, deny, or truncate if you are too quick to stamp it as 'bad' or 'not up to the mark.' Even if it's objectively true, it doesn't take into account all of the other, equally true aspects of the experience. Try to perceive those positive aspects, which you will only be able to discover if you can always stay open to perceive what simply is."

~ SEPTEMBER 2011 ~

When intuition develops, you don't always know why you say and do things differently, but when you are in that divine flow you are in tune with truth. Then, everything goes as it should.

~ **Paramhansa Yogananda** ~
in *Conversations with Yogananda*, #303

LISTEN MORE

*Dear Divine Ma,
What do You want me to learn today?*

"Its time to start listening more to what others are trying to tell you—for your own good. Ask yourself: How often are you able to accept others' criticism as helpful for your improvement? When others offer you suggestions, don't assume that they're just letting off steam. Don't immediately dismiss their ideas as not worth taking seriously. I haven't filled My universe with randomness. There is a purpose in creation.
I am always caring for every soul in My universe.
I give you tests for your growth and learning.
To ignore these opportunities is like drowning in floodwaters and—while waiting for God Himself to help you—ignoring the person in a rowboat who offers you a hand. Remember that I work through instruments. Don't ignore feedback. Listen!"

~ NOVEMBER 2012 ~

WHY MAKE A FUSS ABOUT OTHERS' EGOS?

*Dear Divine Ma,
What do You want me to learn today?*

"Success in life, and on the path that ascends to Me, comes to a very great extent by being loyal, and positive. If you gossip about others, it will spread disharmony. It's time to learn to feel complete respect for others, and to love their souls so much that you scarcely notice their imperfections. Every living person has deficiencies that separate them from the pure qualities of the soul. If the ego were not attached to the body and senses and their heavy physicality, it would cease to be an ego at all; it would be free to soar, knowing itself as a soul without the slightest trace of impurity.

"Because the personality reflects the ego, not yet unalloyed soul, how can it not have egoic imperfections? Of course it does! Every ego does. Every person does. Why make such a big fuss? People are trying the best they can to grow beyond their downward-pulling traits and to know the bliss of the soul."

~ AUGUST 2013 ~

After calling to [the guru] for some time, try to feel his response in your heart. The heart is the center of intuition *in the body. It is your "radio-receiver." Your "broadcasting station" is situated in the Christ center between the eyebrows. It is from this center that your will broadcasts into the universe your thoughts and ideas. Once you feel an answer in the heart, call to the guru deeply, "Introduce me to God."*

~ Paramhansa Yogananda ~
The Essence of Self-Realization, p. 139

THE REAL PROJECT IS WHAT WE BECOME THROUGH OUR ACTIONS

*Dear Divine Ma,
What do You want me to learn today?*

"Your job is to get many people involved, and help them feel a sense of ownership of the project. Your task is delegation—preparing small projects that anyone can do, and *not* to do them all yourself. Remember that they want to feel My love and joy flowing through them as *they* serve, every bit as much as *you* do! This is why you all are serving Me.

"It isn't about making the project successful. *You* are the project. What you accomplish outwardly is not important spiritually, because what you *become* through the project is the project. Remember that it's all about the people. As Swami constantly said, 'People are more important than things.'* Even more important than projects! What we become through our actions is the whole purpose of our efforts. What the project can give people is an enjoyable way to serve Me, and by serving, to know Me. Nothing else matters."

~ OCTOBER 2013 ~

*Swami Kriyananda, *The Art of Supportive Leadership*

IT'S ALWAYS ABOUT GROWING SOULS

*Dear Divine Ma,
What do You want me to learn today?*

"You will find all of the answers you are seeking in love. You are so concerned about getting your projects done. Yet no one cares when the project gets done. They care only about whether they feel loved. Your primary job is to love. Every soul that comes to help you needs to receive your love. *Not* just being treated nicely. Not merely *not* being told what to do, but knowing that you truly care about them, without the slightest judgment. When you were at Ananda Village recently, you made a very valuable experiment of looking at each person very consciously, without letting your mind label them with the traits you had observed in them. It was a fine first effort!

"But you need to take it further. No judging, certainly, but even more is needed: genuine caring, and wanting the very best for the soul standing in front of you. Your life is *not* about getting things done, or growing food. It's always about growing souls. This is the job that few can do. Many can grow food, but bearers of the Light grow souls!"

~ JUNE 2014 ~

What is one to make of personal intuition? Certainly, it exists. Probably no major victory is ever achieved without it. There are people, moreover, who possess this faculty in greater measure than others. The best leaders almost always possess it in abundance, even when they exercise it unconsciously... Nevertheless, if you want to develop them into a team of discriminating and cooperative co-workers ... you had better speak of this impulse to others only rarely. Instead, offer them sound reasons.

~ Swami Kriyananda ~
The Art of Supportive Leadership, p. 63

LET OTHERS BLOSSOM
IN THEIR OWN TIMING

*Dear Divine Ma,
What do You want me to learn today?*

"Be patient with those who may be less
committed than you. They have their own needs,
their own pacing, their own rhythms.
'Tension never helped a tree to grow.'*
Just offer them goodness, and watch how
they will unfold. They are good people.

"They have chosen to come here to help you.
They expect no pay for their work,
and they work hard. Its true that they won't always
be able to 'get with the program' as you would like.
But you, too, love your independence—
you love to figure out how something
should be done, without being told.
Let others blossom in their own way and
in their own timing. They will produce marvelous
fruits that you would never be able to force
from them in a million years. Be at peace!"

~ JULY 2015 ~

*Swami Kriyananda, *Cities of Light*

CHAPTER 3

THE EFFORT TO FOCUS

To receive inner guidance, concentrate at the agya chakra, the point between the eyebrows, which is the sending station for our thoughts. Now ask for guidance from the superconsciousness. You can send out a strong thought like, "What shall I do?"

~ Swami Kriyananda ~
Intuition for Starters, p. 34

HE AWAITS VERY NEAR

*Dear Divine Ma,
What do You want me to learn today?*

"You are making progress! There is much to learn.
Once you sincerely stop resisting My guidance,
nothing will be able to hold you back.
God wants you to be totally open to Him.
That is all you need to know. The way to salvation
is by openness of heart. It's not so much your mind
that needs to open. It's all about your heart.
When you can tangibly feel the Lord's
presence in your heart, all else will be given.
The experience of the Lord is everything you need
in this life. 'Light and shadows of the Lord.'*
Experience them, and delusion will fall
from your eyes. You are not far.
Keep on persevering. Know that He
awaits you very near now. Do not give up.
Seek Him with all your might."

~ OCTOBER 2004 ~

* Paramhansa Yogananda

IT'S TIME TO GET YOUR PRIORITIES STRAIGHT

*Dear Divine Ma,
What do You want me to learn today?*

"You are blessed—blessed to have so many opportunities to think of Me. Why do you spend so little time thinking of Me? You think of the world, with its work and its pleasures, and so seldom do you think of Me. Am I not the origin and goal of all your striving? Is there anything else worth working for than Me? It's time to get your priorities straight. What is it that you most want from life? Is it superficial experiences of the senses and unsatisfying ego gratifications?

"Or is it true, when you say that what you want most is to find God? You *have* found God.
All you have to do now is cling to Me.
I am everything that you are seeking.
Why, then, continue looking elsewhere? I love you.
The only thing missing is your love for Me."

~ OCTOBER 2004 ~

You'll begin noticing that when a certain feeling comes, and you follow it, things work out well. Then there's a different feeling, less calm or clear. At first you may think it's got to be right, but over time you'll come to recognize this feeling as false guidance.

Gradually you'll come to understand the difference from your own experience. You may not be able to explain to others how you know, but when you learn to recognize true guidance, it cannot fail you.

~ **Swami Kriyananda** ~
Intuition for Starters, p. 50

LET GOD BE YOUR ONLY DESIRE

*Dear Divine Ma,
What do You want me to learn today?*

{ Help me, Lord. Help me to find You.
I need Your strength, and Your love. }

"You have Me. I am yours. Where do you imagine
that I have gone when you feel bereft of Me.
To where could I possibly escape?
This world is My own. I made it for you, from
My own being, to 'educate and entertain you.'*
Yes, it's all for your benefit. And yes, the greatest
lesson is to realize that you want Me above
all else in My creation. As long as you find
My creation more enticing than I,
there will still be much to learn.
Let Me be your only desire, then the world
will have fulfilled its role for your life."

~ OCTOBER 2004 ~

* Paramhansa Yogananda

GOD NEVER WAVERS

*Dear Divine Ma,
What do You want me to learn today?*

{ On the first anniversary of our honeymoon,
my wife and I are looking forward to having fun
in a spiritually uplifting environment, in Rishikesh.
And, yes, I do look forward to having the mind
cease its endless wanderings so You can enter.
I would be honored by Your presence. }

"And I would be honored by *your* presence.
Wherever do you think I have been?
I have never moved. I am that I am.
Where has *your* consciousness been?
I never waver. But you, on the other hand, are
like a massive wave—constantly waving.
I am the broad sweep of the ocean, still and steady.
Why do you rise up in opposition to My stillness?
Relax into My vast silent ocean, then you
won't have to struggle so much, and
your life will become pure joy."

~ OCTOBER 2004 ~

I've learned over the years to trust my intuition. As my friend put it one time, "You have a very good track record." It works, and that's why I've learned to trust it. Also, I found out what works and what doesn't work. How the feeling is when it's right and what the feeling is when it isn't right.

~ Swami Kriyananda ~
"About Spiritual Marriage," a talk given Jan. 1981

DO THE WORK, THEN GRACE WILL DESCEND

*Dear Divine Ma,
What do You want me to learn today?*

"It's time to open your heart more fully to receive My love. You spend hours talking about Me, yet little time communing with Me in the secret recesses of your heart. You are missing the ingredient of Love. You are still trapped in your mind. Wisdom is better than ignorance, but it is not the highest expression of My Love. You need to *surrender* to My Love, merge yourself into My Light, My Bliss. '*Ananda*' isn't just the name of an organization; it is the destination of every soul on earth.

"Are you working—putting in the time and effort—and surrendering to My Love that alone can take you all the way to the goal? Why stop short? *Ananda* is waiting for you. You know it's true—you've experienced it. But it won't happen without diligence. Apply yourself to your *sadhana*! Do the work! Then grace will descend. Remember, it's your birthright."

~ FEBRUARY 2005 ~

LIVE NOT FOR WORK, BUT FOR GOD

*Dear Divine Ma,
What do You want me to learn today?*

{ It's been so long since we've spoken together. Yes, I *do* want to be here. I yearn for the solidity of Your presence. I love you, Lord. I want you in my life *so* much. Never let me lose You. }

"How could you lose Me? Am I not always with you? I am the air that you breathe. There is no place where I am not. Allow Me to discipline you."

{ I would be honored. You are my Everything, Lord. I want *only* Thee. }

"Then why do you spend so much time and energy in other pursuits?"

{ But it's mostly in work and service for You, my Lord. }

"Well, that's true. But work and service are not the twin halves of the spiritual path. *Meditation* and service are."

{ True. }

"You need to bring your life more into balance, My child. I want only what is best for you, never anything that would leave you less God-attuned, whole, and fulfilled."

{ Wholeness is good. God-filled is best. }

"Continue to be willing, but be willing to live not for work, but for God."

~ MARCH 2005 ~

Don't wait for some sort of pronouncement, or expect a vision or voice from the clouds, but have the courage to act. By not acting, we often close the door to real guidance, *whereas in the process of acting, the energy begins to flow more clearly.*

~ **Swami Kriyananda** ~
Intuition for Starters, p. 67

LISTEN, AND DO WHAT GOD ASKS OF YOU

*Dear Divine Ma,
What do You want me to learn today?*

"It's time to learn that you are not as important as you imagine. The cosmos does *not* revolve around you and your wishes. You and your wife have your different dharmas. You would be able to see yours more clearly, if you would pay attention and do what you've been told. You listen, but you too rarely do what I ask. The advice I give you is custom-made for you. You are eager to share My inspiration with others but less eager to put it to practice in your life. Will you ignore this counsel, too?

"If you don't act upon what I give you, why do you imagine that I would continue to guide you? If a friend stops listening to you, will you call him again? Our relationship is a two-way street. Energy is needed on both sides. And the same is true with Swami. 'Keep calling Him.'*
Keep communicating. He loves you."

~ APRIL 2005 ~

* Maitri Jones, "Keep Calling Him," a song based on a poem by Paramhansa Yogananda

DON'T RESIST GOD

*Dear Divine Ma,
What do You want me to learn today?*

"I would like you to go to bed earlier. You'll never find God if you can't stay awake during your sadhana. It's no use pretending to do sadhana; you must really go after Me. 'The pearl of great price'* is not for sleepyheads. Get the rest that a real spiritual effort requires. And be sure that you truly want what I can give you. I offer you the universe; be sure that you aren't simply hoping for stale worldly cheese. Invite Me into your life. I can only help you if you don't resist Me. You are blessed *if* you choose to be blessed. I love you. Never forget this."

~ APRIL 2005 ~

* Jesus, the New Testament

Composers have spoken of receiving their inspiration from higher realms: from God, as some of them have put it. Scientists, too, have sometimes had sudden glimpses into the nature of material reality for which they could not account in rational terms. The physicist Albert Einstein stated that the Law of Relativity came to him in a flash. After that experience, he labored for ten years to present it understandably to his fellow scientists.

~ Swami Kriyananda ~
The Hindu Way of Awakening, p. 17

BRING GOD TO LIFE IN YOUR SADHANA

*Dear Divine Ma,
What do You want me to learn today?*

"It's time you began taking God seriously."

{ What does that mean? }

"It means that you must no longer put Me on the back burner of your life; that you must put first things first; that you must no longer put your best energy into useless pursuits, but give Me, at last, the place of honor that I deserve."

{ You're sounding jealous, Lord. }

"Perhaps I am. But if you continue to put other things ahead of Me, even though you *know* how important I am to you, you will never find Me. You aren't doing enough to bring Me tangibly into your life. You talk about Me, but you seldom *invite* Me. What good will it do you to make Me merely a theory? You must bring Me to life in your sadhana. Do it now!"*

~ APRIL 2005 ~

* Swami Kriyananda, *Do It NOW!*

CATAPULT RIGHT OUT OF DELUSION

*Dear Divine Ma,
What do You want me to learn today?*

{ How can I keep going when I feel
my energy winding down? }

"Why aren't you doing the energization exercises?
Why aren't you doing more of what I've taught you?
How can you expect to find God, if you aren't
using what He has given you? You are blessed
to live in the ashram of a great master, with one
of the most blessed souls in the history of the planet.
Are you really willing to let this opportunity
slip by without taking full advantage of it?
This is your chance to get out of delusion!
You can choose to remain trapped in the little body
with its nest of troubles, or you can use this
opportunity to catapult right out of delusion.
Which will you choose? It is *your* decision!"

~ MAY 2005 ~

*Confusion often assailed me,
and doubt—doubt not about
the reason I was here,
but about some puzzling
point in the teachings.
At such times I would sit down
wherever I happened to be,
and try to calm my mind.
For I knew that* soul intuition*,
not intellect, was the key
to real understanding.*

~ **Swami Kriyananda** ~
The New Path, p. 155

USE WHAT THE LORD GIVES YOU

*Dear Divine Ma,
What do You want me to learn today?*

{ Help me to know and to do Your will. }

"You don't have trouble knowing My will! Remember Yoda, the cute little spiritual teacher in the movie *Star Wars*? In answer to Luke Skywalker's protestations that he was 'trying,' Yoda answered, 'Try not. Do!' When will you start doing what you *know*? You listen fine, but seldom do you put into action what you've heard!

"You are storing knowledge like one would into a computer's short-term memory. The knowledge is fine, but unless you *use* it, you will surely lose it. Why risk losing the rich treasure that I have given to you? In the future, your intuition may stop flowing if you fail to use it. Take seriously what the Lord gives you—act upon it unhesitatingly. Don't leave it moldering on the shelf."

~ JUNE 2005 ~

PROVE HOW MUCH YOU WANT GOD

*Dear Divine Ma,
What do You want me to learn today?*

{ I've had difficulty making contact with You lately. }

"Yes, it's time to change your approach."

{ I'm hardly ever really trying. }

"To achieve your goals, you must put out more energy, willingness, and enthusiasm. Do you still want to find Me?"

{ Yes, I do, but I too often want God to come without risking that I will get tired, or that I'll be inconvenienced in any way. }

"But you seek 'the pearl of great price'! How can you expect to earn something of such inestimable value without working hard for it? God *is* attainable, but not by sluggards. You must *want* Me. Only then, when I know that you are sincere, can I let Myself be known. You must *prove* that you want My presence. Then I will come!"

~ DECEMBER 2005 ~

A very great error occurs when people insist—as some have done—that any personal effort to commune inwardly with God is fraught with spiritual danger, for it leads to self-deception. This error is allied to the belief that divine communion— *which is, certainly, a grace of God— is in no way the result of human effort ... As well might one say that nothing can be done to bring sunlight into a room, when the only obstruction to it is the fact that all the window curtains have been drawn shut. God certainly wants us to commune with Him. It is we who shut Him out by our restlessness, material desires, and dull indifference.*

Meditation is, in fact, the best way of removing all mental obstacles.

~ Swami Kriyananda ~
Revelations of Christ, p. 60

MAKE TIME FOR GOD

*Dear Divine Ma,
What do You want me to learn today?*

"If you're feeling that you need My presence in your life once again, why aren't you spending more time with Me? One or two meditations a week plus your three or four ten-minute pseudo-meditations at lunchtime are *not* going to get you there. You need to make Me your highest priority again. You know what to do. You know how to do it. And if you truly value My presence in your life, you will make the time.

You make time for other things that you consider important. Am I less important than those outward projects? Isn't it selfish, egotistical, and downright self-centered to hold Me at bay? Wouldn't you like to be God-centered again? Let's change these habits together, shall we?"

~ MAY 2006 ~

GOOD DEAL?

*Dear Divine Ma,
What do You want me to learn today?*

"It's time to take more seriously your need for sadhana. Why not dedicate this entire month to an experiment? See what progress you can make this month by having longer sadhanas. Try it for just one month and see if it kills you. Then decide if your old habits are making you happier than your sadhana. Make a limited, one-time trial—a grand experiment. It won't be a major change in your life, not a revolution, just a brief experiment in an attempt to discern My higher truth.

"Find out which brings you more happiness and joy—your habits, or your prayers and meditations? If a month-long trial fails to prove that sadhana is a more powerful source of happiness, go ahead and return to your old habits. Good deal? Replace the few minutes that you use for your old, time-worn habits with more sadhana, then gradually and naturally increase the time you spend in sadhana, and see what happens."

~ JULY 2009 ~

Think, "There is an answer, and it will come to me."... When we energetically offer our thoughts to the **superconscious** *level with confidence that the answer will be there, true guidance readily comes.*

~ Swami Kriyananda ~
Intuition for Starters, p. 36

GIVE FROM YOUR HEART, NOT ONLY YOUR HEAD

*Dear Divine Ma,
What do You want me to learn today?*

"The lesson today is to care. Bless others with your love. Love others in tangible ways. That is, express your love tangibly, so that others can feel it. Don't be guilty of 'faith without works.'*
Give from your heart, less from your mind. Make your faith practical. Without giving My love actively to others, not even feeling My love in your heart is enough. Feeling and action are both required. Faith without works is dead. To *act* spiritually is more important than simply to *feel* that you are spiritual. Don't let the feeling of love make you forget the need for action, lest the spring of love dry up.
Love must be expressed; it must be made practical. 'May I be able to awaken Thy love in *all* hearts.'"†

~ OCTOBER 2009 ~

---

* Jesus, the New Testament
† Paramhansa Yogananda, *Whispers from Eternity*

IF YOU ONLY PERSEVERED A BIT LONGER

*Dear Divine Ma,
What do You want me to learn today?*

{ Please help me to take my spiritual practices more seriously. It's difficult for me to be always present, awake, and energetic. }

"The energization exercises would help—of course. As would going to sleep at the appropriate time, and reading spiritually uplifting books, apart from your news magazines—not exclusively, but not to be neglected. You've become lazy. It's time to start putting out spiritual energy again. We miss you! You sit in meditation, but you don't stay and try to make a real connection. Seldom do We see you penetrating the darkness with your consciousness to touch the level on which the Divine can be known. If only you would persevere a little more!"

~ JULY 2011 ~

*Can we really attract
inspiration at will?
Yes indeed! Strong energy,
powered by confidence . . .
can attract inspirations,
opportunities, solutions
to problems—anything . . .*

*But it's important that
faith not become an excuse
for irresponsibility. To live
superconsciously means
to cooperate with the
superconscious flow,
not to expect that flow
to do everything for you.*

~ Swami Kriyananda ~
Awaken to Superconsciousness, p. 250

SADHANA IS NOT FOR WIMPS

*Dear Divine Ma,
What do You want me to learn today?*

"It's all about patience and forbearance.
Are you able to keep going forward, even when
your circumstances seem bleak and nonproductive?
Are you willing to slog through the difficult times,
or will you be merely a fair-weather friend?
The spiritual path is not for weaklings!
You must really want transformation with all
your being. The growth that comes from sadhana
is not for wimps. A great deal of tapasya—
of spiritual discipline and self-sacrifice—is involved.
Are you ready to do what it takes?
Do you have the patience to let the seed unfold?
Persistence is needed."

~ DECEMBER 2012 ~

SMALL STEPS AT A TIME

*Dear Divine Ma,
What do You want me to learn today?*

"Make God your only reality."

{ That seems too huge, Ma! There's still so much of life that I am interested in. }

"Oh, but most of your interests now are God-reminding. Yes, there are a few movies, magazines, a little radio listening, and your ten minutes three times a week on the Internet. Not much else is left to distract you from Me. But perhaps you could turn two of your three news magazines into spiritual reading, and devote every other night to spiritual reading. That would help draw your thoughts to Me and God. Why not try it? One news magazine is sufficient to keep you informed. And they don't inspire you. Use more of your time to be inspired! Then I will be more nearly your only reality. Small steps at a time are enough."

~ JANUARY 2013 ~

*It's more than surrender.
I had that before. It's more
than listening to God.
I tried that before...
It is an act of will.
I compel my mind to open
straight out toward God.
I wait and listen with
determined sensitiveness.*

~ **Frank Laubach** ~
Letters by a Modern Mystic, p. 9

WHAT DO YOU WANT— SLEEP, OR SAMADHI?

*Dear Divine Ma,
What do You want me to learn today?*

"It's time for you to take your search for Me more seriously. You seem to think it's a game, where you can devote fifteen or twenty minutes and feel virtuous. Well, that simply isn't going to get it done. If you are serious about wanting to find God, that level of effort won't do it. You need to 'double down,' as they say. You seem surprised that I know what's going on. Nothing astounds Me. But people can disappoint Me. As when I see individuals with the true spiritual potential to go all the way languishing contentedly without making the effort that would bring them ultimate fulfillment. What *do* you want? Sleep, or *samadhi*?"

~ FEBRUARY 2013 ~

DO YOUR DHARMA NO MATTER HOW INCONVENIENT

*Dear Divine Ma,
What do You want me to learn today?*

"It's time to work on perseverance."

{ Really? I would have thought that I had a superabundance of it, almost too much stubborn "stick-to-it-iveness," to ask for more. }

"No, stubbornness isn't what's needed. You need to continue to follow dharma, no matter how inconvenient, difficult, and personally uncomfortable the task might be. For example, in your sadhana you have begun to listen to your lesser inner citizens, the ones who are urging you to do what's easy and comfortable for your body. They came close—very close—to knocking you out of your sadhana two days in a row. This is a dangerous trend. Perseverance means doing your dharma no matter what. And everyone needs more of *that* quality."

~ JULY 2013 ~

*One of the best things we can
do with our life is to become
a positive force in the world,
to be filled with love, joy,
and compassion, and eager to
nurture others. Merely asking
the question, "What would God
want me to do in this situation?"
can profoundly improve our
lives and the lives of others.*

~ Nayaswami Jyotish Novak ~
How to Meditate, p. 111

THE LIGHT ALONE SUSTAINS THIS WORK

*Dear Divine Ma,
What do You want me to learn today?*

"Perseverance pays! When you keep at your meditation, it will give you everything you *need*—and sometimes even what you *want*. As you well know, Self-realization is not a question of putting in a coin and expecting a bottle of bliss to pop out. You must persevere, and you must deeply want it. It's no good to go through the motions, doing your meditation practices mechanically.

"Transformation is not for quitters—it's for spiritual heroes. You already know how to serve, but do you know how to give yourself completely? To give not only when it's convenient, but also when it isn't, if someone really needs your help? True love doesn't count the cost; it weighs the need and rushes to meet it. As Asha remarked, 'That is what a Lightbearer does.'* We bear the Light to those who lack it, and we show them how they can receive the Light for themselves.

*In a private conversation with the author

"The Light is the only thing that keeps
this work afloat: not theology, not service,
not meditation practices, not individual intelligence,
not classes, altars, events, money, buildings,
or projects—not even in this case people.
The Divine Light alone sustains this work.
It would be good to remember that *true* sustainable
farming is done with the consciousness of
the Divine, guiding each act we do."

~ JANUARY 2014 ~

RESTLESSNESS

*Dear Divine Ma,
What do You want me to learn today?*

"Finding Me requires stillness. You can never come close to Me unless you are willing to cultivate perfect stillness inside. You are always in motion—
too often, commotion! I am waiting for you to be sufficiently still so that I can get through to you.
But you are seldom still enough to receive Me.
I want to talk to you—to love you—to uplift you—
to inspire you. But your mind is so often elsewhere.
How can I touch you within, when you so often are without? You're moving too fast for My thoughts to catch up with you. Yet you can draw Me so simply, by just asking, 'Hello God, are You still there?'
That will surely work. But you must remember
to ask—*and to listen* to the answer!"

~ AUGUST 2015 ~

CHAPTER 4

OVERCOMING THE EGO

*When the heart's feelings
are like a flawless lens,
intuition unfolds like a blossom
and brings* clarity *to all
one's perceptions of reality,
revealing things as they
truly are and not as delusive
desires may have painted them.*

~ Swami Kriyananda ~
The Hindu Way of Awakening, p. 220

A TREASURE TO BE CHERISHED

*Dear Divine Ma,
What do You want me to learn today?*

"Get yourself out of the way. It's time to demand
that your little ego turn away from the body's
pestering interruptions. You have experienced God.
It's time now to ignore the body's demands.
Why do you cling to old, familiar ways?
Why not instead allow yourself to be blessed
by God's transforming Presence? To the extent
that you experience Me and then act as if nothing
had happened, you denigrate the Spirit.
These are sacred truths that have been
entrusted to your safekeeping. Do not carelessly
gloss over what the Lord has entrusted to you.
These sharings are a sacred treasure to
be cherished. Act accordingly!"

~ DECEMBER 2004 ~

IS SATAN REAL?

*Dear Divine Ma,
What do You want me to learn today?*

"I want you to learn how to focus, not only your energy, but your devotion. You seem surprised when you realize that I am listening to your thoughts. But who do you imagine is directing you to the right path in everything? I am your own conscience. I am all that is best in you. If you would only listen to Me, rather than that 'sad fellow on your other shoulder.'"*

{ Who is Satan; is he real? }

"Oh, yes. Satan is a force that you must actively oppose in thought and action. Otherwise, if you remain passive, you will quickly fall into his clutches."

{ Why do You allow Satan to exist? }

"If Satan didn't exist, why would anyone want to find Me and know Me as I am? People yearn for something better in life only because they have tasted pain and suffering, from following that other fellow."

{ Why does Satan exist? }

* Nayaswami Haridas, Sunday sermon

"To motivate people to choose Me."

{ Is he . . . part of Your team? }

"Of course! Nothing exists in this universe, without My sanction. I make and unmake sextillions of worlds at will. I will that Satan exists only to help people turn toward My Light."

{ But so many get lost in suffering and despair, owing to Satan's influence. }

"No, they suffer because they make wrong choices. How will they learn, except from their own experiences? If turning the right way gave them no better result than turning the wrong way, who would care which way they turned?"

{ But so many turn the wrong way. Why don't more choose the right way? }

"Because of My power of delusion, which makes the temptations of this world appear attractive at first, though painful later. The path to God is 'narrow and steep,'* as Swamiji's song puts it. And the 'pearl of great price'† is rare, and difficult to attain."

~ DECEMBER 2004 ~

* Swami Kriyananda, song, "The Philosopher and the Boatman"
† Jesus, the New Testament

First of all, to recognize the kind of feeling that indicates true guidance, look for three qualities: calmness, clarity, and joy... If it makes you feel emotionally excited, then it probably only reflects the temporary happiness that comes when our desires are fulfilled. True guidance should have a joy that takes you inside rather than outside of yourself.

~ **Swami Kriyananda** ~
Intuition for Starters, p. 48

IT'S ONLY YOU AND GOD

*Dear Divine Ma,
What do You want me to learn today?*

"God enters in and fills the void when the ego with its endless desires has finally dissolved. As long as the ego and its desires reign supreme, God will take a backseat in your life."

{ Yes, I need more of God in the pilot's chair of my life. }

"There isn't room for both King Material Desire and King Soul to occupy the throne of your life.* You must choose. You must fully recognize the gnawing feeling of emptiness, aloneness, and abandonment that is the underlying truth of human existence. If you cannot face it, you are deluding yourself, living in a fantasy world of your own imagining. We are all ultimately alone. In your life there is only you and God, no other. In truth, there is only God. God alone†.

To hope for anything else is delusion. And as long as you are waiting for happiness to come from any other source, you are bound to experience only suffering."

{ Help me, Lord, to throw myself into Your arms alone! As Swamiji writes, "I've grown tired of strangers' songs."‡ }

~ MAY 2005 ~

* Paramhansa Yogananda, *God Talks with Arjuna*   † Gyanamata, *God Alone*
‡ Swami Kriyananda's song, "I've Passed My Life as a Stranger, Lord"

KARMA STICKS ONLY TO THE EGO

*Dear Divine Ma,
What do You want me to learn today?*

"It's time you began to set aside childish games. You are no longer an adolescent. Act like an adult for once. See how, each time you allow the ego to take hold of you, it makes you selfish and unhappy.

"As long as the ego wins, you create karma that you'll eventually have to work off, because karma sticks to the ego. Wrong habits of the ego are like a hitching post that holds your life in bondage. Untie your life from that post of ego, and your whole mental state will be free. No more selfishness, no more fears, no more burning disappointments over unmet expectations and attachments. Attachments need something to attach themselves to. Give them the slip. Give less importance to the little, whining ego. Stop thinking of the body as home and bad habits of selfishness will find no point of attachment and simply drift away. All selfishness and pain comes from attachment. Learn to let go of attachments, and live in this world as a free soul."

~ APRIL 2006 ~

*You can be sure that your
guidance is wrong when you're
too emotionally involved, because
your desires have interfered
with your ability to be clear
and objective ... The powerful
emotional energy of our likes
and dislikes is a strong force
in overriding real intuition ...
If the heart's feelings are
already biased by personal
desires, then the outcome
is predetermined.*

~ Swami Kriyananda ~
Intuition for Starters, pp. 84–85

BURNING THE CANDLE AT BOTH ENDS IS SELF-DEFEATING

*Dear Divine Ma,
What do You want me to learn today?*

"Nothing bad will happen to you as you learn to renounce old sense-born habits. Fear not; you are not alone in the struggle to master the senses. The happiest people are not the most self-indulgent—despite their empty boasts! Rather, the happiest are those who are finding God through renunciation."

{ Do sense habits get in the way of finding God?}

"Of course they do. You can use your energy at the top of the spine, *or* you can allow your energy to spill out through the senses at the bottom of the spine. But you can't attain My all-desire-quenching bliss if you burn the candle at both ends."

~ JULY 2009 ~

ONLY GOD BRINGS UNENDING HAPPINESS

Dear Divine Ma,
What do You want me to learn today?

"God alone is sufficient to bring you the lasting happiness you are seeking. Why search for it elsewhere? Everything else is a dead end, and never satisfies for long. Only God will never disappoint you. Money, intoxicants, sex, fame, power—all break their promise and end in boredom. Even the best marriages end in death and painful separation. What of these can bring us a happiness that is unending? None! Only God! 'Let nothing disturb you, nothing affright you. All things will pass, but God changes not . . . Once you have God, you'll want nothing more.'"*

~ AUGUST 2009 ~

---

* Swami Kriyananda, "St. Teresa's Admonition," a chant based on the writings of St. Teresa of Avila

Can we really attract *inspiration* at will? Yes indeed! Strong energy, powered by confidence (which must be rooted in faith; it must not be ego-confidence), can attract ... anything.

It isn't a question of wanting anything, personally, but of wanting it because it is right. It is important to exclude ego-motivation as much as possible.

~ Swami Kriyananda ~
Awaken to Superconsciousness, p. 250

DO YOU REALLY WANT TO INDULGE THE EGO?

*Dear Divine Ma,
What do You want me to learn today?*

"It's time to bring more balance into your life. You must be careful to take appropriate time for work *and* play, the spiritual *and* the personal. If you give too much time to work, your human ego will rebel."

{ Hmm, that's true. }

"It's only the ego that wants 'free' time. The soul is happy to serve."

{ Interesting! }

"But if you push too hard on the 'work' side, the 'play' side will rebel and fight back."

{ Yes, like yesterday. But what will I gain if the "play" side wins—and I fall into low-energy activities that don't uplift my consciousness: watching videos, over-eating, and so on. Do I really need more of those? }

"Only your ego does. Why should you indulge your ego's wishes? Do you really *want* to strengthen the ego?"

{ *No!* }

~ NOVEMBER 2009 ~

PAY MORE ATTENTION TO GOD HIDING BEHIND NATURE

*Dear Divine Ma,
What do You want me to learn today?*

"It's time to listen to the birds. When do you take time to enjoy nature's beauties all around you? Nature is a beautiful aspect of My creation, yet you notice it for at most perhaps three minutes per week. You devote perhaps sixty minutes per week to your worst habits. Yet you spend so little time enjoying the beauties of My creation. Is that fair? No wonder you're becoming a bit cynical. Open your eyes and ears to the beauty all around you, and give less attention to the ugliness.

"The world can be a grand place if you give it a chance. President Theodore Roosevelt—who championed the National Parks movement—would have noticed nature's beauty singing and shimmering, and he too was a busy man. No use hiding behind the excuse of 'busy-ness'! Pay more attention to Me hiding in the glories of My Nature."

~ MARCH 2011 ~

"At the moment you are pilgrims and need only your daily marching orders, and strength and *guidance* for the day. Oh! Listen to My voice, eagerly, joyfully. Never crowd it out. I have no rival claimants, [but] if men seek the babble of the world, then I withdraw."

~ A.J. Russell ~
God Calling, Jan. 11

A FREE SOUL IS MERELY ONE FREE FROM EGO

*Dear Divine Ma,
What do You want me to learn today?*

"It's time to realize that Swami is not going to give you what you *want* in this lifetime. His role is to give you what you truly *need*. If he were to cater to your desires, it would only strengthen your ego. When your desires are finished, there will be nothing holding the ego together. Your soul will be free.

"Ego is the only barrier standing between you and the bliss-filled state of freedom. What is there to fear in letting go of ego?"

{ That's right. Fear alone prevents me from knowing God's bliss, fear expressed through repulsion, reaction, dislikes, and their opposites—attraction, desires, and likes. }

"When you can learn to still the restless emotional feelings of the heart, as Patanjali says, you will find freedom from the likes and dislikes that prevent you from knowing Me. A free soul is very simply one who is free from all taint of ego. Then, truth is seen clearly and there is nothing to fear, nothing to desire but that which exists at the heart of everything—God's all-satisfying bliss.

"Having transcended likes and dislikes, there is no longer anything separate to aspire toward. *Yogas chitta vritti nirodh*—'Yoga is the neutralization of the vortices of feeling.' This is the journey's end. When you can achieve that perfect poise of heart, nothing stands between you and God: *satchidananda*—ever-existing, ever-conscious, ever-new bliss."

~ MAY 2012 ~

THE EGO DOESN'T WANT TO GIVE UP

Dear Divine Ma,
What do You want me to learn today?

"Its time to give yourself—all of yourself!—into God's hands. It's time to open yourself completely to My guidance, My will, and stop following your own will. Does it frighten you? Are you fearful of losing control over your life? I understand. That is merely the ego fighting your good resolve, and hoping to keep you in its thrall. The ego doesn't want to give up its domain.

"But if you want to receive freely from My hands, you must turn away from the ego's whispered suggestions. The ego will refuse to give up trying to tempt you until, as with Bhishma in the Mahabharata, it decides that it's time. You cannot make the ego give up until it is ready. Don't worry, there is nothing to fear, for nothing can ever be taken forcibly from the ego. It will only give in when it realizes the wisdom of surrender. No one can force the ego."

~ JANUARY 2013 ~

When you allow the mind to become restless with thoughts and desires, then you bring yourself down to a level where God can't communicate *with you.*

~ Swami Kriyananda ~
A Handbook on Discipleship, p. 50

AS LONG AS YOU'RE ATTACHED TO ANYTHING, GOD WAITS

*Dear Divine Ma,
What do You want me to learn today?*

{ What do you want me to work on for the new year? }

"Above all, it's important that you be honest with yourself. Let others think what they like: their opinions don't matter. But are you hiding anything important from God? He already knows your habits and proclivities. Just remember, desires fulfilled strengthen the ego."

{ Can I find God if I still have an ego? }

"It's very unlikely. God requires that we give Him *all* of ourselves. As long as you are attached to anything else, He will wait."

{ But I see the light sometimes, hear the AUM, feel God's joy, sense the power, feel breathlessness and deep calm. Do I need to perceive more than those to know God? }

"Those experiences are merely a first step. You must open your whole being, without reservation. God will turn you inside out and fill you completely when He comes. These first perceptions are just precursors to that great transformation."

~ JANUARY 2013 ~

FOLLOW DHARMA ALONE, NOT EGO DESIRES

Dear Divine Ma,
What do You want me to learn today?

{ You are so slippery—I think I have You, but then You're gone. }

"I know, but I am always with you."

{ I do feel alone sometimes. }

"Only when you turn your back on Me and try to go your own way, making your own decisions and ignoring My advice."

{ I rarely take Your advice. }

"I've noticed that. Why is that?"

{ I think it's because I want to feel that I am my own man. }

"Ah, you mean your ego wants to be the leader in your life. Your ego doesn't want to give way to dharma. But this is why you would find it very difficult to work with A——. Your ego wants to do everything your own way. You are attached to your own agenda, and therefore inattentive to the wider good of the souls who make up the Sangha. Make dharma alone your guide—not the little ego's petty desires!"

∼ AUGUST 2013 ∼

> First, we must try to *empty* our
> consciousness of ego, and then
> to refill it in a divine way...
> I'm not setting myself apart.
> I'm trying to say,
> "Look, anybody can do this!"
>
> ~ **Swami Kriyananda** ~
> *Music, Creativity, and Superconscious Experience,*
> a talk on June 19, 1996

LOVE IS ABOUT GIVING

*Dear Divine Ma,
What do You want me to learn today?*

"Today I want to talk about love. When will you finally be ready to understand that it's perfectly fine to express true devotion, or love, toward another human being? Not praise that merely flatters the person's ego, and should be shunned by souls intent on enlightenment, but My true, impersonal kindness and compassion.

"You are learning to separate love from sex. You formerly thought that they came as a matched pair, but it was never true. It is humanity's greatest delusion, thinking that if they get more physical intimacy, they will feel more loved. And yet as Jesus said, the comforts of delusion 'last hardly an hour.'* In truth, love has nothing to do with sex. If love were not separate from sex, what old couples would stay together?

"Love is the highest refinement of feeling in the human heart—completely free of neediness or a wish to take, but imbued only by a longing to give. Love is a giving. Love is an overflowing feeling of expansion from the heart that embraces the other person. That compulsion to seek sex is something else entirely: lust."

~ AUGUST 2013 ~

* Swami Kriyananda's song, "To Souls That Were Fallen"

FEAR OF THE LIGHT

*Dear Divine Ma,
What do You want me to learn today?*

"You need to persist if you want to find My Light between your eyebrows. You give up too easily."

{ Is it laziness, or is it fear of failure? }

"It is fear of the Light! The Light asks you to let It transform you, and you still aren't fully convinced that it's what you want. Transformation means that you must be prepared to let go and leave behind your favorite mental citizens— the tendencies in your personality that separate you from Me. You cannot enjoy the lures of a lower consciousness, and expect to know Me.

"As in Swamiji's book *The Land of Golden Sunshine*, you aren't yet sure that it's better to strive to know Me and My Bliss, if it means forsaking the sense comforts that you have become accustomed to. As Asha often says, 'Clinging to your bad habits just means that you get to keep them!'"*

~ APRIL 2014 ~

* Paraphrasing Richard Bach, author of *Jonathan Livingston Seagull*

CHAPTER 5

LOVE, DEVOTION, AND SURRENDER

Spiritual advancement isn't a question of attaining anything, really. It is only a matter of opening wide the door to a state of conscious being that is ours already, hidden from us only so long as our attention is focused elsewhere. As, by regular meditation, the door gradually opens, ego and soul are able to work in closer cooperation together.

It's fascinating, and I can't explain it well, but it's as though there were two "me's" carrying on; and more and more frequently they seem to get through to each other.

~ Swami Kriyananda ~
"How Should We Relate to You, Swami?",
in *In Divine Friendship*, p. 166

DEVOTION: THE OIL THAT SMOOTHES THE SPIRITUAL QUEST

Dear Divine Ma,
What do You want me to learn today?

"I have missed you. Where have you been of late? You show up so seldom. Even when your body is present, you too often leave your heart—your devotion—behind.

It is not enough to do the techniques in a perfunctory manner, and then run away. In your meditation, always take time at the end for inner communion. This world is crying out for love. Don't let your meditations be like the world, bereft of loving. If you truly want to lift your spiritual life out of the doldrums, the only remedy is love.

"Devotion is the oil in the machinery of the spiritual quest. Without devotion, your efforts to find Me are fruitless, barren. When you meditate, never go through the motions mechanically; it is dangerous, and much more so because it can so quickly and easily become a habit. If you confine your efforts in meditation to merely 'showing up,' without giving it every last drop of your heart's energy, why would you expect to receive a heart-filling response? Be in love with the Divine, then your efforts can bear fruit."

~ NOVEMBER 2004 ~

LET YOURSELF GO INTO THE LIGHT

*Dear Divine Ma,
What do You want me to learn today?*

{ What is the right way to approach my sadhana for the near future? }

"Just keep opening yourself to go deeper and deeper every day. If you would only surrender and let Me in, you would be amazed. Let each cell of your body be transformed by My touch. The Light wants to take you in. In his play, *The Land of Golden Sunshine*, Swamiji tells us that it is a blessed, sacred event when you can let yourself merge into the Light. Don't hold anything back. You have become too body-conscious—getting more exercise will help you rise above the body in your meditations.

"Fear uncontrolled desire, not the exercise routines that can help you rise above My creation. Lifting weights at the gym can help, but walking is even more important. Be blessed by the sun and the birds and the air. All nature is filled with My being! Take time to appreciate what simply is!"

~ NOVEMBER 2004 ~

"Practicing the presence of God has already been proven by countless saints. Indeed, the spiritual giants of all ages have known it. The results of this effort begin to show clearly in a month. They grow rich after six months, and glorious after ten years. This is the secret of the great saints of all ages. "Pray without ceasing," said Paul. "In everything make your wants known unto God. As many as are led by the spirit of God, these are the sons of God."

~ Frank Laubach ~
Letters by a Modern Mystic, p. 90

GIVE LOVE FIRST TO OTHERS

*Dear Divine Ma,
What do You want me to learn today?*

"It's time to start being more fully open to what your life wants to be—to your divinely appointed dharma. You've become a little set in your ways—wanting to accomplish everything with your own reason and will, instead of listening intuitively for My guidance, and acting with love. Start opening yourself to the influence of My love. It is I who am speaking to you. I am the only source there is. Unless you truly love Me, how can I make Myself fully known to you? I long to give you more of My love. But you will only be able to receive it if you are willing to open your heart and express your love for Me. In order to receive My grace, you must first open your heart and give. This is the spiritual law. There is no other way to receive My love unless you first open your heart *by giving love to others*, and then give that love to Me."

~ DECEMBER 2004 ~

PUT GOD FIRST

*Dear Divine Ma,
What do You want me to learn today?*

"It's time to start putting God first. 'Seek ye first the kingdom of God and His righteousness, and all these things shall be added unto you.'* Are Jesus' words true? Why not test them and find out for yourself? Make Me the sole focus of your life. Otherwise, what's the point? You cannot grow spiritually unless you make Me the focus of all your thoughts each day. Let Me be the core and center of your life— the light in your eyes each morning, and each evening. When you interact with others, let them feel they are interacting with Me. I am everything you need.

"But if you ignore Me—forget to love Me—what can I do? When you draw Me by your love, you open the channel by which I can give you My love. Don't let worldly preoccupations prevent you from thinking of Me. You *must* put Me first. Until you do so, desires for this and that will continue to imprison you, and you'll experience only misery."

~ FEBRUARY 2005 ~

* Jesus, the New Testament

*I do not advise you to use
a lot of words in these prayers.
Many words and long discourses
are just opportunities for your
mind to wander. Do this instead.
Hold yourself before the Lord.
Remain there as a poor man sitting
at a rich man's gate:* waiting.
*Let it be your business to keep your
mind in the presence of the Lord.*

~ **Brother Lawrence** ~
Practicing His Presence, p. 81

A DAILY INVITATION

*Dear Divine Ma,
What do You want me to learn today?*

{ It's wonderful to return to morning group meditation.
I don't do as well when I meditate on my own.
How can I draw closer to You, Lord? }

"Make time to seek My presence within you.
Until you find Me, how can you feel close to Me?
Read My *Whispers from Eternity*. Dive into
the heart's innermost feelings of devotion to Me.
Chant alone every evening—it will help you.
Let Me know that you love Me. If you don't
take time to express your love for Me, how can you
even be sure that it's what you feel? You will be blessed
only to the extent that you 'open your heart to Me.'
Only then can I 'enter and take charge of your life.'*
Don't let your sadhana become an empty ritual;
it's a daily invitation. Only you can make it real."

~ FEBRUARY 2005 ~

---

* Paramhansa Yogananda, quoted in Kriyananda's *The New Path*

CONDUCT THE EXPERIMENT

*Dear Divine Ma,
What do You want me to learn today?*

"Let others know that you care about them. They want to feel your love. Spend more time chanting and meditating; that's the focus of this teaching center: chanting and meditating; loving God individually and finding Him together. There is only one way to happiness and freedom— by 'loving the Lord with all thy heart, with all thy mind, with all thy soul, and with all thy strength; and thy neighbor as thyself.'* This is the heart of the Law and the essence of true religion. Nothing else is needed but love. If you can't yet believe it, conduct the experiment. Love others, and see if it works. Once you've tried it for an extended period, you will know."

~ MAY 2005 ~

---

* Jesus, the New Testament

*Don't think of
tuning in to intuition
as receiving answers
from some prophetic voice
from on high, but rather
as listening sensitively
to the whispers of your
own higher Self.*

~ **Swami Kriyananda** ~
Intuition for Starters, p. 63

JOY IS YOUR BIRTHRIGHT

*Dear Divine Ma,
What do You want me to learn today?*

"Work selflessly. That is when you're making the most rapid progress toward God. You are His child; ask of your Heavenly Father whatever you really need and it will be given. How can your Father refuse you? You are His very own. There is no question of His love for you. The only unanswered question concerns how much you love *Him*."

{ It seems so mercurial, up and down. }

"Love Me, Love Me, Love Me—and all your fears, all your sorrows, will pass away. Joy is your birthright. Claim it as your own. It 'awaits you in your own Self.' "*

~ MAY 2005 ~

---

* Swami Kriyananda, Ananda's Festival of Light

YEARN FOR GOD

Dear Divine Ma,
What do You want me to learn today?

{ Lord, reading the book of Ramakrishna's quotes[*] has moved me deeply. I want to want what he wanted. He was a true lover of God. He was blessed, by his own attitude of receptivity, to know the Divine Mother. Master, I long to desire You that much. How can I learn to want You that much? I know that You are everything, but I need to pull You out of the ether by my devotion. I yearn to yearn for You, my Lord. I need to melt my heart. It is I who am frozen, cold of heart, incapable of summoning the love and yearning that would freeze You into a form that my consciousness can perceive. I want to open my heart and weep for You. Help me, Master, to have that kind of love for You. I am Your servant. Ask of me Your bidding. }

~ MAY 2005 ~

---

* Mahendranath Gupta, *The Gospel of Sri Ramakrishna*

*Remain persistent,
undepressed, through
dark and seeming silence.
If in the midst of life,
disease, and death
you play the dancer,
yet* **keep calling** *Him,
you will receive
His answer!*

~ **Paramhansa Yogananda** ~
From the song "Keep Calling Him"

MERE HUFFING AND PUFFING DOESN'T MAKE CONTACT

*Dear Divine Ma,
What do You want me to learn today?*

"Be open to My presence. Look into My eyes. If you want to find Me, get devotion! Your approach has been *so dry* of late. Don't you know that I am 'the most relishable,'[*] as the Bhagavad Gita says? I want only what is best for you, nothing else. But if you don't reach out to Me, I cannot come to you. Don't you know that I am present in your every thought of Me? This is why I tell you, 'Open your heart to Me, and I will enter and take charge of your life.'[†] You *must* think of Me, look into My eyes, and love Me if you want to know My response in meditation. Kriya Yoga without devotion is just huffing and puffing. You must make contact!"

~ SEPTEMBER 2005 ~

[*] Krishna, the Bhagavad Gita
[†] Swami Kriyananda, Ananda's Purification Ceremony

YOU'RE ON THIS EARTH TO MANIFEST LOVE

*Dear Divine Ma,
What do You want me to learn today?*

"It's time to learn to love. Truly to love! As in loving others without considering what's in it for you. If you want to know Me, there can be no attachment to the fruits of your labors. *None!* Why not learn to love simply because it's the right thing to do for your own happiness, and not because it might make you look good in other people's eyes, or because you feel virtuous in doing so? Not because it might balance those actions you think are less admirable? The simple fact is that, in reality, you *are* love. Every other feeling is a delusion, a corruption, a falling-away from the consciousness you have come on earth to manifest."

~ OCTOBER 2009 ~

*Pray to God
mostly in your own words
of love and yearning,
not in the borrowed
language of others.
Never cease to keep up
your prayers to God
until He answers you.*

~ **Paramhansa Yogananda** ~
How to Be Happy All the Time, p. 143

THE ONLY CONSTANT IS YOUR LOVE FOR GOD

*Dear Divine Ma,
What do You want me to learn today?*

"Your idea of a balanced life is no longer working. It's time to recognize that you've changed, and you're different than you were. Have these changes come about with advancing age? Or is it a question of your health, karma, genetics, or diet?

"Whatever the cause, your life—your energy!—is not what it used to be. Your limbs are compromised. Your body needs more sleep. Your waistline keeps bulging. Your singing practice is sporadic, your voice less reliable. You are forgetting simple things. How long before you can't remember your social security number? You've lost the ability to remember dates and even some appointments. And yet, this can be a positive time of change, a time for growing into a new and better reality. The only constant must be your love for God. Everything else will change, but your desire to open your heart to God must not change!"

~ JULY 2011 ~

KNOWING GOD LOVES US IS ALL WE EVER NEED

*Dear Divine Ma,
What do You want me to learn today?*

"Just love! Is anything else more important? Love is the only thing that every person longs for. Once you *know* that you are loved, you'll find that nothing else is missing, truly. We look for human love when we aren't sure that God loves us. Once we know that God loves us, due to our own experience of that love—in meditation—its 'all we ever need.'* Isn't it?

"The 'great leap' that we all long for is to know the experience of that love, in *nirbikalpa samadhi*: the unbroken, irreversible state of union with its sole source. We have had glimpses of that presence that take our breath away. But then worldly consciousness returns again and again. How will we find that deepest point of consciousness where nothing returns but God? God alone!"†

~ SEPTEMBER 2011 ~

* Swami Kriyananda, "St. Teresa's Admonition," a chant based on the writings of St. Teresa of Avila
† Gyanamata, *God Alone*

This year I have started out to live all my waking moments in conscious listening *to the inner voice, asking without ceasing, "What, Father, do you desire said? What, Father, do you desire this minute?" It is clear that this is exactly what Jesus was doing all day every day.*

~ **Frank Laubach** ~
Letters by a Modern Mystic, p. 4

YOU WERE MADE FOR LOVING

*Dear Divine Ma,
What do You want me to learn today?*

"It's time for you to learn to be more big-hearted. Don't allow others' behavior to contract your heart. You were made for loving—love is what you are. If others are unable to give their love, give them the freedom to be who they are. But don't let their narrowness constrict your giving. Be yourself, without censure or resentment, and without dampening the feelings of your heart.

"Your loving nature is one of the best features you possess. Let it shine! You can be dignified and centered in your love, like G——, but do make the effort to connect with others. Be demonstrative; reach out to them and be interested in their stories. There is so much loneliness, insecurity, and confusion in the world. You have a confidence and a life-wisdom that can help many. True, only those who are ready will be able to receive. Many are lost in self-doubts and pride. But for those who are drawn to you, you can serve them as a guide. I want you to make yourself available to others. That is how they get to know Me, by feeling My presence in those who, like you, are devoted to Me. Stand in My love and others will feel it."

~ MAY 2012 ~

GENUINE CARING

*Dear Divine Ma,
What do You want me to learn today?*

"We want you to learn to open your heart to each person you meet. You serve as a representative of Ananda, and through your example they will discover what Ananda is like. If you care about the people you encounter, they will feel loved by Ananda. If they feel that someone from Ananda cares about them, it will leave them with a favorable impression of Ananda. Like it or not, you are among the few public faces of Ananda in your city, and as they view you, they will view Ananda.

"Don't be pretentious—trying to present an unnatural or exaggerated image of Ananda. Just be yourself—there is no value in hypocrisy. But genuine caring will be an inspiration to others. Be real. Be non-attached. Be centered 'in the spine.'* But also be warm. Always remember that a true yogi, no matter how inwardly detached from this world, is always ready to serve as an instrument for My love."

~ AUGUST 2012 ~

* Paramhansa Yogananda, *How to Be Happy All the Time*, p. 128

Do away with the mockery of mechanical, loud praying. Shake off the false satisfaction of believing "just something" about God. You must know God. *You must know how to rouse Him consciously.*

~ **Paramhansa Yogananda** ~
the original *Yogoda Lessons*, 1925, pp. 2–4

IT ISN'T THE DOING THAT MATTERS: IT'S THE BEING

*Dear Divine Ma,
What do You want me to learn today?*

"The spiritual life is entirely about attunement. You know what to do; what counts most is *how* you do it: the right feeling, the *bhav*, with which you do it.

"It isn't the doing that matters; it's the *being*. The consciousness with which you act is everything; the actions themselves matter much less. The only actions that truly matter are those you do with the highest consciousness. What is high consciousness? You can think of it as acting with My presence, if you like. That, too, is right action.

"Where is your mind when you're acting? You can do almost anything, yet as long as you are in tune with My consciousness, you could become a saint in the doing.

"Put your mind on Me. Give yourself to Me. Open your heart to Me, and you will see that all else is fluff. If you act with your mind fixed on Me, on God, your actions will *be* those of a saint.

"It really is no more difficult than that. We love to make the spiritual path complicated, when it's really all just a very simple question of right attitude—the direction of your thoughts and feelings. If you keep your mind churning with thoughts of Me, or the Father, or the Guru, where else will your thoughts take you but to Me? God is everything you have ever wanted."

~ JUNE 2013 ~

WITHOUT LOVE, WHAT IS WORTH SHARING?

*Dear Divine Ma,
What do You want me to learn today?*

"It's all about love. If you don't have love in your heart, for Me, for your spouse, for the person you are teaching, for the people you lead, then what do you have that is worth sharing? Without love, what is *worth* sharing? Buildings are everywhere—they can't make anyone wise or inspired or uplifted. The objects and activities that people crave on the material plane don't change them in positive ways. Spiritual progress is always about the heart. Do you really care for the other person? If not, they will go where they *do* feel cared for.

"There is never enough caring and true loving in this world. That is something of great value that you are able to provide. Short of loving, everything else about your work can be done better by specialists. Only loving people will persuade them to want to stay."

~ AUGUST 2014 ~

You can find God in the solitude of your own room when, in the early morning hours and before sleeping, you compose yourself for meditation.

With folded hands say mentally, "Father, Thou art omniscient. Thou knowest my every thought. Talk to me. I want to hear Thy voice." Say it mentally again and again until you feel it. You have to culture this feeling, to work for it.

Repeat the prayer again and again until you find that your heart throbs with love and yearning for God, and you get a conscious response.

~ **Paramhansa Yogananda** ~
How to Be Happy All the Time, p. 142

YOU HAVE TO WANT GOD SO MUCH

*Dear Divine Ma,
What do You want me to learn today?*

"This is a big day.* It's one chance in the year to break through your resistance to merge with Me. No, it's true! And it's going to be harder this year, since your family commitments mean you'll have to leave early. But realization doesn't so much take time, as it takes depth and persistence. Depth is far and away the most important goal. Simply hanging on isn't enough. You must deeply desire to merge with Me—to be firmly attached to it. You have to *want* God so much that you would give up all other desires to accomplish that single 'desireless desire.' Only by merging yourself in Me will you find the fulfillment you've always been seeking.

"Don't meditate for show, or for carving notches in a stick. You can't get realization by having a certain number of *sabikalpa samadhis*—as if you were trying to win a sports tournament. Only by self-offering, and by surrendering your ego to My will, once and for all, will your heart become truly, and finally, free."

~ DECEMBER 2014 ~

* Ananda's annual eight-hour Christmas meditation

SEE ONLY THEIR SPIRIT

*Dear Divine Ma,
What do You want me to learn today?*

"It's time to open your heart to others, and to Me. Your heart is troubled by worries, emails, rules and regulations. Just tell your heart to stop, be calm, and take time to think of Me. If you make your main prayer very simple— 'How can I love You more?'—you will be able to get your project up and running in the right way. Keep asking me, 'Hello, God. Are You still there?' And then listen for My answer. That is the way to remain in tune and openhearted. Bless others by focusing only on their spiritual potential, not on their deficiencies or bad habits.

"Everyone has bad habits, but the most important thing is where their heart is. What are their souls' intentions? How much do they love? Your best strengths don't lie in knowing how to grow better, nor in your practical expertise. But you can give your *love!*"

~ JULY 2015 ~

CHAPTER 6

GOD IS THE DOER

Babaji stated that Jesus Christ had appeared to him and declared, "What has happened to my religion? My followers are doing good works, but too many of them have forgotten the essence of my message of direct, *inner communion* with God. Let us together send again to the West the secrets for achieving that communion."

~ Swami Kriyananda ~
Revelations of Christ, p. 141

REALIZE THAT GOD IS THE DOER

*Dear Divine Ma,
What do You want me to learn today?*

"It's time to let go of the feeling that you must do everything yourself. It *is* time to realize that *God* is the Doer. Why keep pushing so hard with the little self? Get God, then let Him act through you. You are not the Doer. You never were. When you try to make things happen by your own power, you only get in the way of how they are meant to unfold. That which is trying to happen can only manifest when your take your little self out of the way and let the true Self accomplish what It alone can do. The fruits of oneness with the Self are harmony, calmness, peace, joy, wisdom, and power. You will never find them in the little self."

~ SEPTEMBER 2004 ~

SEE GOD IN EVERY SOUL

*Dear Divine Ma,
What do You want me to learn today?*

"It's time to start looking at each one of your brother and sister disciples—at each being—everyone!—as a manifestation of God. It's so important to see Me in every soul, or else you'll miss recognizing My presence all around you. Bless each one as if you were seeing Me, which is indeed true if you will only see clearly. I am omnipresent. I am that I am. You must develop the clarity of vision to perceive Me everywhere. Once you are able to see, you will know that there is no place that I am not. Then the world will become 'dowered with divinity.'* It's a beautiful phrase, and it's true. To clear your sight, the only thing necessary is to love."

~ NOVEMBER 2004 ~

* Paramhansa Yogananda

*Dear sister in Christ,
you do not have to "go to church"
to be in the presence of the Lord.
You may come to Him by yourself.
Learn to express your heart as
you turn to the Lord within.
Speak to Him. Speak with meekness,
humility and love. Anyone is
capable of a very close and
intimate dialogue with the Lord.
It is true, some find it easier
than others. But remember,
the Lord knows that fact, too.
So begin. Now. Be daring!*

~ **Brother Lawrence** ~
Practicing His Presence, p. 72

ACKNOWLEDGE THE POWER GREATER THAN YOURSELF

*Dear Divine Ma,
What do You want me to learn today?*

"I want you to learn to go deep in meditation. It isn't enough just to show up; you must *want* to find Me! If you don't want Me with all your heart, why should I come? It's not as if I don't have other things to attend to. Realize what a tremendous blessing it is when I reveal My presence to you. If you imagine that it's like the passing of an ordinary moment, how can you imagine that I will bother to return? It *is* a very great blessing! There is only so much that you can do on your own.

"Until you realize that there *is* a power greater than yourself in this universe, there will always be sharply curtailed limits to what you can accomplish. This is why the *Vishwarupa* in the Bhagavad Gita is so important. Once you have *genuinely acknowledged* My power in the universe, nothing will be able to stop you."

~ DECEMBER 2004 ~

DON'T FORGET THAT IT'S GOD ACTING THROUGH YOU

Dear Divine Ma,
What do You want me to learn today?

{ Help me to focus on You. I want to love you with all my heart. What is holding me back? I am distracted by so many things, all of them pressing for my attention. How can I begin to act as if God truly mattered? I need to find clarity about that. Perhaps I have been too lazy and sleepy. I am not yet truly devoted. And I do want to be. Speak to me, Lord. I want to do what You want me to do. }

"It's time to serve with *Me* in your heart. Too often you imagine that it's *you* who are doing the acting. You forget that it is I who act in all things through you, and that it is *I* you are serving.
If I am omnipresent, how can you act apart from Me? When you serve, remember that, as your Guru said, 'God is serving God.'*
That is the nature of his drama."

~ JULY 2005 ~

* Paramhansa Yogananda, quoted in Swami Kriyananda's *The New Path*

The direct way to attune ourselves to superconsciousness is by meditation. The essential attitude for correct meditation is one of listening. *The difference between prayer and meditation is that in prayer we talk to God, whereas in meditation we listen for His answer.*

~ Swami Kriyananda ~
Meditation for Starters, p. 23

THE FINAL CHALLENGE

*Dear Divine Ma,
What do You want me to learn today?*

"Be open to all of the ways I can come to you. Don't you know that I am present in every one of the interactions of your life? If God is omnipresent, as you believe, how can there be any situation where I am not? The blessed see Me in all things, in all people, in all situations—the good, of course, but also the bad. Once you can perceive My presence even in negative situations, you will see Me everywhere. Then it can be said that you know God. You already *know* God, both through these 'listenings' and by the fruits of your sadhana. Now you must learn to recognize Me on the street, in the laborer, in the shopkeeper—everywhere. Once you learn to see Me there, you will perceive Me even in the people who are obstructing your work. *That* will be the final challenge."

~ JULY 2009 ~

THEY ARE YOUR KIN—ACT ACCORDINGLY

*Dear Divine Ma,
What do You want me to learn today?*

"I want you to learn patience. You expect so much from so many—everyone feels pushed by you. Yet they only want to feel loved, not pushed."

{ What can I do to love more? }

"Try caring—truly caring for them. When they speak, *really* listen. Listen behind the words, to the feelings they are expressing, to the mood. Listen to their hopes and fears. Above all, try to open your heart to the truth that they are, quite literally, the children of God. Their Heavenly Father is God, just as yours is. Their mother is Divine Mother, too. Remember that they are My children, as much as you are. You are brothers of one blood, one Spirit. You truly are family. Why treat others as strangers, if they are, in fact, your nearest kin? Cultivate this feeling in your heart, then act accordingly."

~ NOVEMBER 2009 ~

He begins to insist through your own conscience that this is important—those recurring things that come again and again where you feel like I'd really better pay attention to this... That personal roadmap—that path that is right for us—will be different for each one of us. But we have to develop the ability to hear what [the] Master is saying to us. It's based on the whispers of eternity... that play through the conscience.

~ Nayaswami Jyotish Novak ~
Ananda's Inner Renewal Week lecture, Feb. 21, 2018

EVERYTHING IS POSSIBLE WHEN GOD IS THE DOER

*Dear Divine Ma,
What do You want me to learn today?*

{ The pace has been quite hectic of late.
Will I be able to keep up? }

"You forget to remember that it isn't you who are doing your work, but that I am doing it through you. Your job is to get out of the way! Whenever you feel exhausted, it's because you're thinking of yourself as the doer. No wonder you feel exhausted! No human could do what you have been doing. It is not humanly possible. And that's the point, isn't it? When you understand that God is the Doer, everything becomes possible and you don't feel tired all the time. Your fatigue is due to wrong thinking, not too much work. With God, you can do anything!"

~ NOVEMBER 2009 ~

THERE CAN BE ONLY ONE LEADER IN YOUR LIFE: YOU OR GOD

Dear Divine Ma,
What do You want me to learn today?

"Just be. Don't push so much. Learn to listen! What do people need? You don't have to decide or try to make it happen. They will teach you what is needed if you listen closely enough. Open yourself to My guidance. I am always with you. Won't you pause for a moment, and listen to see if I will guide you? I want to guide your life, but you must be willing to follow.
If *you* are always leading, how can I help you? There is room for only one leader in your life. You alone must decide—will it be you, or Me? Whom will you choose as your leader? If you continue to push ahead, I will hold back out of My respect for you. I have no wish to force you to follow Me. This relationship only works if you really want it. Do you? If not, it's all right. I will wait."

~ AUGUST 2011 ~

I am well aware of the probability of criticism because it is "mysticism"— or because many people think that the days of direct contact with God, or at least words from God, stopped with the closing of the New Testament.

~ **Frank Laubach** ~
Letters by a Modern Mystic, p. 42

YOU WILL FIND ME WAITING FOR YOU

Dear Divine Ma,
What do You want me to learn today?

{ You are so great and all-encompassing. It is difficult to lift my consciousness into the realm in which You exist. }

"No: not 'exist,' but where you can perceive Me. Yes, you are often unable to concentrate long enough to perceive Me. But that does not mean that I am difficult to find. It's only that you are sluggish in your efforts. I am present at all times, everywhere. Why do you imagine that I am remote? Am I not always with you, as I was with Anthony in the desert?* You erect mental barriers that keep Me out. But I want to come in. I want to be perceived by you. I live to comfort you. But it is you who hold Me at bay. Lift your mind even a little, and you will find Me waiting for you. I am always here for you. Fear not, I will never leave you. I know every thought that you think, so hold nothing back. I am nearer than your thoughts, closer than your desires. You cannot escape Me even if you try, for I am your own. I am your own Self. There is nowhere you can go where I am not."

~ SEPTEMBER 2011 ~

* St. Anthony of the Desert, in *Saints That Moved the World*

YOU CAN'T LET THE IDEA OF GROWING OLD GRAB HOLD OF YOU

*Dear Divine Ma,
What do You want me to learn today?*

"Your energy is flagging. Is it time to start energizing again? You stopped with the excuse that you had more energy than anyone else you knew. But that is no longer true. Eight years in India have beaten a great deal of energy out of you. How will you get it back? There is so much more that you can accomplish, if you can summon the energy you once had. Will you be content to close down?

"It's true that you have 'given at the office.' But will it be good for you spiritually to 'close shop,' do less, and just take it easy? S—— stated very forcefully that as we age we cannot let the idea of being old take hold of us. To allow that thought to take root in your consciousness would be the end of your spiritual growth. You are *not* your body! You are a child of the Infinite!* Let no thought place limits on what you can accomplish for God and Guru. They will give you all the energy you need, if you cooperate with them. They are your divine lifeline."

~ DECEMBER 2012 ~

*Paramhansa Yogananda, *Autobiography of a Yogi*

"Swami Kriyananda was feeling a strong *inner commandment* from his master to edit the book, Whispers from Eternity. Swami was literally editing the book faster than I, his former secretary, could type. It was as if Master was telling him on the spot just exactly what [to write]."

~ **Asha Nayaswami** ~
Sunday sermon, Feb. 14, 2016

LET THE DIVINE FLOW THROUGH YOU ALL THE TIME

*Dear Divine Ma,
What do You want me to learn today?*

"I want you to learn humility."

{ Has that been a problem for me? }

"Only to the extent that you think people owe you respect. You are beginning to be proud of what you can do with the music. That is not a healthy trend! Better not to do it at all than to become proud of it."

{ But isn't turning our backs on our own talents merely another form of egoism? }

"It's best to be self-forgetful while offering yourself to Me, so that I can act through you. Think of the part of Swamiji's song that says, 'Yes, its She, the Divine Mother.'* Take time to remember that, in your deepest heart, you only want to be in awe of Her,

---

* "*The Divine Mother,*" set to the melody of "Au Font du Temple Saint" from *The Pearl Fishers,* by Georges Bizet

never of yourself. The higher Self alone deserves awe. The Divine Mother does everything through you. You of yourself can do nothing. God does all things through you. Remember this. Whenever you felt that Swamiji was singing through you, you got the songs exactly right. That is true humility.

"It's not about doing less, or hiding your talents, but allowing Me to flow through you, just as Swami did unfailingly. People too often accused him of being egotistical in his actions, and in the delight that he took in his accomplishments. But he was by no means being guided by ego; he was able, far beyond the ability of his critics, to allow Me constantly to flow through him, in My full power. That is what made him Self-realized—that he gave himself so completely to the Self within."

~ JULY 2013 ~

LISTENING TO WHISPERS FROM ETERNITY

*Dear Divine Ma,
What do You want me to learn today?*

"As you hoped, you could call this book *Dear Divine Ma: Listening to Whispers from Eternity* or *Conversations with the Soul.* Yes, that would be nice. But whom are you speaking to?"

{ It's intended only for disciples of this path. }

"No! It is for devotees of any path who love God and are open to the possibility of finding His active presence in their lives—be they Buddhists, Sufis, charismatic Christians, yogis, New Thought seekers, disciples of Unity, Religious Science, CSA/E, Marian Catholics, or Kabbalah Jews. This book belongs to all who want to find their own inner communion with Me through meditation and devotion. All of these might be open to the conversations we've shared in these pages. It has been as much a joy for Me, as it has been edifying to you. We are equally blessed to have had these moments together."

~ OCTOBER 2013 ~

We felt all unworthy and overwhelmed by the wonder of it, and could hardly realize that we were being taught, trained, and encouraged day by day by Him personally, when millions of souls, far worthier, had to be content with guidance from the Bible, sermons, their Churches, books and other sources. Certainly we were not in any way psychic or advanced in spiritual growth, but just very ordinary human beings.

~ **A.J. Russell** ~
God Calling, Introduction

BABAJI IS BEHIND YOUR PROJECT

*Dear Divine Ma,
What do You want me to learn today?*

"It's time to learn to be more humble.
Try to give up wanting to take credit
for whatever happens in the project.
Remember that it is My work, not yours.
God and Guru are watching over our project.
It was never you who made any of this happen;
it was Babaji, working behind the scenes.
How else could so many miracles happen?
We're on the same team. Remember that
no one person can take charge of the energy
and consciousness that I am manifesting
through you all. You can ride the energy like
a surfer on a surfboard, but don't imagine
that you can lead it. It is God's work.
It is His project. You are the stewards
and caretakers, but the blueprints
are in His hands."

~ OCTOBER 2013 ~

BRINGING HEAVEN ON EARTH

*Dear Divine Ma,
What do You want me to learn today?*

"Today you need to remember that I am. That's enough—just remember that *God is*. Once you know that, in every cell of your being, then you will act accordingly."

{ "Behaving As If the God in All Life Mattered" was an important book title. If only more people had taken that concept seriously. }

"Yes, I matter. When people act as if God didn't matter, and only their own decisions, desires, and needs are important, God gets left out of the picture. Yes, I matter. Remember Me, and all will happen as it should. Forget Me, and *that* is Hell. Remembering Me is all it takes to bring Heaven on earth."

~ FEBRUARY 2014 ~

God is Eternal Silence. To those, however, who love Him purely, He speaks through the voice of silent intuition. As their reward for long years of hardship in renunciation, He fills the cup of their consciousness with the ruby wine of Bliss, slaking the age-old thirst of their souls for joy by granting it to them in **direct communion** *with Him.*

~ Swami Kriyananda ~
The Rubaiyat of Omar Khayyam Explained, p. 26

WHAT ISN'T FILLED WITH GOD?

*Dear Divine Ma,
What do You want me to learn today?*

"It would be a good idea to take yourself more lightly. Don't take yourself and your role in life so seriously. You are here to serve. Only that. When you truly understand that God is the Doer, you will understand why it isn't necessary to take everything so seriously. I am here. I simply am. There is nothing that is *not* God. Show Me anywhere where God is not! You worry so much about whether this or that project will be finished, or is good enough, or is God-filled. But consider: what is there in this world that *isn't* filled with God? Once you can see that—truly know it—your life will be filled with nothing but bliss."

~ AUGUST 2015 ~

CHAPTER 7

INTUITION OF GOD'S WILL

The *Cosmic Song* is hidden behind the multitudinous little noises of your own voice and the voices of material noises. The "still small voice" is never silent, but it cannot be heard for the clamor drowning it.

~ **Paramhansa Yogananda** ~
the original *Yogoda Lessons*, 1930,
Super-Advanced Course, 12-3

IGNORE MY WHISPERS OF INTUITION AT YOUR PERIL

*Dear Divine Ma,
What do You want me to learn today?*

"Your only job in life is to follow My will. Every other course will only bring you pain and suffering. Unlike humans, the animals don't add to their suffering by rebelling against My will. The tiger's dharma is to kill and eat, so no suffering comes to the tiger from those actions. People, on the other hand, are free to wander in directions counter to God's will, and those are the actions that bring us suffering."

{ How can we know God's will? }

"You know it even now. You know it because you are listening to My counsel."

{ True, but so few try to hear the inner whispers, or believe them when they do. }

"Yes, even you! There have been times when you have ignored My whispers of intuition, at your peril. Where do you think those calm, wise intuitions come from? It is My voice, showing you the path that would actually work in your life. Don't you think that your life would go more smoothly if you followed My guidance?"

~ FEBRUARY 2005 ~

LISTEN SENSITIVELY

*Dear Divine Ma,
What do You want me to learn today?*

"Inner guidance is *everything*! You cannot know God's will without following intuition."

{ So then, are the concepts that Swamiji teaches us, about intuition, inner guidance, doing God's will, and following our dharma all the same thing? }

"Yes."

{ Then why do even our best teachers seem to back away from teaching others to rely on this guidance? }

"Because people can only learn by having their own experiences."

{ How can one tell without a doubt that the guidance they are following *is* God's, and not their own subconscious egoic thoughts? }

"You've learned by your own experience to feel the difference. Based upon your own experience you are able to discern the level from which your inspirations are coming."

{ How can we teach that skill to others? }

"Teach them to *listen sensitively*, as Swamiji taught. Help others to learn to calm their heart and listen with impartial feeling. If people could learn to do this, the world would be a better place."

~ FEBRUARY 2005 ~

*Everybody can learn
to hold God. And when God
is ready to speak, the fresh
thoughts of heaven will
flow in like a crystal spring....
What a gain if everybody
could rest in the waiting arms
of the Father, and* listen
until He whispers.

~ **Frank Laubach** ~
Letters by a Modern Mystic, p. 81

FINE-TUNE YOUR RECEIVER

*Dear Divine Ma,
What do You want me to learn today?*

"To do well at sadhana, you do need seven hours of sleep. Why not make a point of going to bed earlier, so that your meditations—and your life—will be successful? How long has it been since the Lord came to you tangibly? You are starved for contact with the Almighty. Yet He awaits you around every corner of your life.

"Let Him into your consciousness. It is not His presence that is lacking; there is something wrong with your 'receiver.' You must fine-tune your receiver—the Lord is all around you; if you make your heart receptive, He will come. He has never left you. He is closer than your very thoughts. Let Him in! Let Him make Himself known to you. He is waiting patiently for you to tune your antenna to His frequency. He yearns for you to discover your oneness with Him."

~ MAY 2005 ~

GET QUIET ENOUGH TO HEAR

*Dear Divine Ma,
What do You want me to learn today?*

"It's time to focus deeply on your own dharma—
your divinely appointed role in life. You often
seem to avoid doing what I ask. Yet, what else do
you need to be happy, except to do My will?
Open your heart and feel what I am asking you to do.
Ask of Me, 'What's trying to happen here,* Lord?'
I will guide your actions through your own intuition,
with far better results than you could ever achieve
by your own thoughts and plans and desires.
Don't confine your asking to this journal—ask for
My guidance in every situation, minute by minute,
and you will know what needs to be done.
There is so much wisdom that I can give you,
if you will just get quiet enough to hear it."

~ JULY 2005 ~

* Stephen Gaskin, quoted by Swami Kriyananda

*You must know how to... make
God answer your demands.
Do not rest until you have heard
His voice consciously.*

~ **Paramhansa Yogananda** ~
the original *Yogoda Lessons*, 1925, pp. 2–4

WHEN YOU LEAVE DHARMA, YOU CREATE KARMA

*Dear Divine Ma,
What do You want me to learn today?*

{ It's been awhile since we talked, Ma.
Are you still there? }

"Of course, I'm still here! You keep forgetting, Dear One, that I never leave you. There is no thing that can make Me stop watching over you. But where do *you* keep going? No harm can befall you, so long as you remain in dharma. When you leave dharma, you create karma that will simply have to be re-experienced and overcome in future. It's as simple as that. Don't be selfish with your affections. All love is from Me, and is given to be shared with all, not just those of whom you approve. Imagine how much more constricted and unhappy this world would be, if only those who escaped your judgment were permitted to blossom. Love *all*!"

~ MAY 2006 ~

BY THEIR FRUITS YE SHALL KNOW THEM

*Dear Divine Ma,
What do You want me to learn today?*

"It's time to learn that it's futile to evangelize people who don't want your help. Answer their questions, but never force your ideas on them. They will find it very unappealing. Give them the right, the courtesy, to remain ignorant—even unaware that you might actually know something in this field. Does it matter what they think of you? Their opinion of you is 'none of your business.'* All that matters is your love for Me."

{ But how *can* I know that it's You, and not my own subconscious—or even Maya, 'the Devil'—that is speaking to me? }

"'By their fruits ye shall know them.'"†

{ Yes, that's true. When I do what You say, it has a way of always working out. The other voice has often failed me. It was selfish, and uncaring of others. }

"Yes, judge them by their fruits . . ."

~ FEBRUARY 2008 ~

* Asha Nayaswami, Sunday sermon   † Jesus, the New Testament

[*The* Essence of the Bhagavad Gita *manuscript*] is being given to me. Nothing I have ever written has flowed so easily. I pray, and the words are there… I typed it out as it came to me. This is not my book. It is Master's…

Inspiration comes to those who are humble about their own achievements and reverential toward the achievements of God.

~ Swami Kriyananda ~
quoted by Asha Nayaswami, in *Swami Kriyananda As We Have Known Him*, p. 280

THE STILL SMALL VOICE WITHIN

*Dear Divine Ma,
What do You want me to learn today?*

"It's time for us to talk about love. Not mere human love, but love for the Divinity in each one. I am He. I am in every cell of every body. Who is loving whom? 'God is helping God.'*
We can do nothing of our own, but only with the power lent to us by Almighty God, the force of life and goodness that is within you and within Me. What is it that silently whispers the right thing to do, the good thing to do? That is God within you. To the extent you follow *that* whisper (and there are others), you cannot miss. True lasting happiness, real joy, is what results from listening to what some call, 'the still small voice within.'† Listen for that."

~ SEPTEMBER 2009 ~

---

* Paramhansa Yogananda, quoted in Swami Kriyananda, *The New Path*
† Jesus, the New Testament

DOWSING FOR THE DIVINE

*Dear Divine Ma,
What do You want me to learn today?*

"You are a blessed being. So is every one, especially when they realize what they were made for. Each of you is 'dowsing for the Divine.' Our hearts are antennas to receive divine instruction, for guidance, and for the motivating power to act. Without the divine signal, we would stop dead in our tracks. We may think that we are living, but our life as we tend to live it is delusion. Our life is given to us so that we might tune our consciousness to the only signal that ever truly matters. All else is distraction. 'God alone'* is real."

~ OCTOBER 2009 ~

* Gyanamata, *God Alone*

*The mind must suspend
its normal activity
of analyzing, of
weighing alternatives,
and of generally
"talking" so much that
one cannot hear [what]
the superconscious
is [saying].*

~ Swami Kriyananda ~
Meditation for Starters, pp. 23–24

WHAT CHANNEL ARE YOU TUNED TO?

*Dear Divine Ma,
What do You want me to learn today?*

"Help Me to feel that you love Me, not for My gifts but for My being. You spend so much time doing this meditation technique or that good deed. But how often do you think of Me? If, as you say, you are doing all of these things 'to find God,' wouldn't it be more useful to say hello to Me once in a while? Or at least think of Me on occasion? Remember 1987, when you delighted in saying very simply, 'Hi, God. Are You still there?' And I would always answer you right away. Wasn't that fun? It was a delight for both of us. Let's do that again during the coming months. I am not so far away.

It's your consciousness that is far from Me. I don't mean your worldly thoughts. Yes, those, too, at times. But I am more concerned about the direction your mind is turned.

D—— was correct when she challenged you all by demanding, 'What channel are *you* tuned to?'* You alone can choose to attune yourself to Me. Your level of joy and happiness depends entirely on which of the many possible channels you choose to attune yourself to. Why waste time on those lower frequencies? Come up to *Joy*!"

~ OCTOBER 2011 ~

* Nayaswami Dhyana, talk at Ananda's Spiritual Renewal Week, Aug. 1995

DHARMA OR DRAMA?

*Dear Divine Ma,
What do You want me to learn today?*

"It's time to learn what makes people tick. Why do they do what they do? What motivates them? They are motivated by a desire to feel worthwhile, or, above all, by a desire to find happiness. If they feel good about themselves, or just plain feel good, they'll repeat the actions that caused them to feel that way. People either feel good about themselves from their conscience, or they feel good from their senses. Often, those two ways to happiness evoke actions that are diametrically opposed. Dharma leads to feeling good in one's higher Self. Drama is feeling good in one's lower self, the little ego. Dharma or drama? That's what motivates people: their conscience or their senses. They are moved to seek happiness in one way or the other. Anything less leaves people without sufficient motive power to get them going."

{ We each must *want* to act. We need a sufficient reason to go beyond inertia. It has to feel good enough to stop doing nothing. Paramhansa Yogananda said that boredom is man's habitual state. It takes no energy to stay bored. Getting the energy moving, therefore, is the first, and hardest, step. }

"So, get your energy moving!"

~ MARCH 2012 ~

*I am finding every day that
the best of the five or six
ways in which I try to keep
contact with God is for me
to wait for His thoughts,
to ask Him to speak.*

~ **Frank Laubach** ~
Practicing His Presence, p. 15

TOO SELDOM DO YOU SIT LONG ENOUGH

*Dear Divine Ma,
What do You want me to learn today?*

"It's time to learn to be the man you are destined to become. It has been a long time since you allowed Me to move through you daily, as your life's partner. You used to go for walks while inwardly chanting a favorite mantra—'I love you, Swamiji!'—and you would become so inspired by My presence. But you don't do it anymore, and it would help you immensely to open yourself in that way again.

"You too seldom take time to access Me through this journal, and you too seldom sit long enough—as you finally did in yesterday's meditation—to see the spiritual eye clearly. These are the doorways by which you can ask Me to enter and transform you into the man you were meant to be. I yearn to come into the world through people like you. But you must take the first step.

I am ready and eager to help you. Yet for months you've failed to show up. It is not hard. It is not difficult. It's a question purely of whether you are willing."

~ APRIL 2012 ~

ARE YOU TRANSFORMING YOURSELF?

*Dear Divine Ma,
What do You want me to learn today?*

"Its time to tune in more receptively. Are you truly open to Swami's guidance? After his last scolding, it took you many long months to open your heart again. Then he 'let you go' from his building project a year ago, and you still haven't completely forgiven him.

"How open is your heart to his influence? How open are you to what *I* tell you? You record My answers faithfully in your journals, but then why do you forget to apply it to yourself, keeping it mostly for the instruction of others? When will you act on the guidance I give you? Why should I continue to offer My wisdom, if you only ignore it? Are you willing to put My guidance to the use for which it was intended? Do you truly want to be transformed?

"Merely listening to this counsel can *begin* to change your consciousness. But oh, I long for you to go farther! and actually put My counsel to use!"

~ NOVEMBER 2012 ~

I knew that I was in touch with the same Power that inspired the great poets, and also Bach, Mozart, and Beethoven. Then the ideas...flowed in upon me with such force and speed, that I could only grasp and hold a few of them; I never was able to jot them all down; they came in instantaneous flashes and quickly faded away again, unless I fixed them on paper.

The themes that will endure in my compositions all come to me in this way ... I felt that I was, for the moment, in tune with the Infinite, and there is no thrill like it... Those "visitations of my celestial patroness," to quote Milton, are my most precious memories.

~ **Johannes Brahms** ~
in Arthur Abell, *Talks With Great Composers*, p. 69

JOY IS THE DIVINE BAROMETER

*Dear Divine Ma,
What do You want me to learn today?*

"The true gauge of your life's worth is not your accomplishments. It's joy. If you are receiving joy—*not* merely pleasure, but true Joy—from the service that you are giving to the world, then you can know for certain that you are in dharma—that you are living in the right way. Joy is the divine barometer. Whenever your joy increases, it means that more of God is flowing through you. I believe that you want as much of God flowing into you as you can bear. When you are living in God, all the other little pleasures fade away. How seldom do we find ourselves living in God, thinking of Him, talking to Him, seeing the inner beauty that is His, and most of all, listening to Him and His guidance for us. He has all the answers we ever need—He even has all the questions! There is nothing truly worthwhile that He is not. In fact, there *is nothing* that He is not! Try to find a spot, or a corner, or an activity, or a person, where God is not present. It can't be done. In truth, He is omnipresent. All is God. All is One. All is Love."

~ FEBRUARY 2013 ~

I WANT YOU STRONG WHEN YOU TACKLE YOUR NEXT MISSION

*Dear Divine Ma,
What do You want me to learn today?*

"I am here whenever you're willing to listen. I will tell you whatever you need to know. If I told you what job you were supposed to take, you'd miss the joy of discovering it within."

{ Yes, but what if I head off in the wrong direction again? }

"Then you will have to stop and listen for My inner guidance until you get it right."

{ I'm listening now. Can't you save me the time? }

"Sure, but then it would come too easily, and you wouldn't grow. I want you to be strong when you tackle your next mission. It will be a doozy."

{ Ah, Lord, but I went off chasing windmills on Your behalf, and my loyal wife almost got crushed by the experience. Shouldn't I wait to see what she feels she needs to do, and support her in her intuition, rather than dragging her along once again? }

"Perhaps with the right intuition, you'll both find a path to serve Me that is nurturing. That is what I want for you."

~ MAY 2013 ~

*In working with the book
The Essence of Self Realization,
I could actually* hear *Master's
voice in my mind, talking,
and completing these sentences.
Now I can't ask you to believe it.
I can simply tell you that
this is what I believe and know.
But it was so. And from then on,
I resolved that I wanted to
spend the rest of my life
letting Him tell me what to do.*

~ Swami Kriyananda ~
Sunday sermon in Palo Alto, March 5, 2000

LASTING JOY IS WHERE DHARMA LIES

*Dear Divine Ma,
What do You want me to learn today?*

"Success in everything requires a clear mental focus. Focus on the right things! Choose dharma, the right, divinely-guided action, in everything. And then let nothing dissuade or divert you from that resolve. When you know the right thing to do, do that, and that alone. Feel blessed to know what's right and wrong. Many people are unable to discern the difference. But you can, when your own desires aren't blinding you to the truth. As in the movie *Mistress of Spices,* you have the power of intuition, but desires can easily pull you away—they blind you to the truth. Remain focused on what is true—on those things that bring not transitory, but lasting joy. That is where your dharma lies."

~ APRIL 2014 ~

JOY AWAITS YOU IN BLISS

*Dear Divine Ma,
What do You want me to learn today?*

{ Was that Jesus today? }

"We* are all there!"

{ Really? }

"All of the time.
"We are always present, merely waiting for some brave, loving souls to open their heart to us enough so that we might 'enter, and take charge of your life!' When some person really opens up their heart enough for that to happen, that is what makes *nirbikalpa samadhi*, the Oneness that never leaves, unending Bliss. We all want each of you humans to experience that. If only you didn't all cling so to your little habits, your confining egos. Don't you know how much joy awaits you in Bliss?"

~ APRIL 2014 ~

* Referring to the gurus of Self-Realization—Jesus, Babaji, Lahiri Mahasaya, Swami Sri Yukteswar, Paramhansa Yogananda, Divine Mother, God the Father— and to all saints and saviors of the planet

*"How sweet the sound of Om,
It's Master's voice I hear.
In all-pervading silence,
He whispers, 'I am here.'"
Dr. Lewis wrote that song from a place of pure expanded consciousness. That's how that came to him. When he had attuned himself to the Divine, he could hear the whisper in his heart. The [same] way that God will speak to us if we are quiet enough—if we get still enough to hear it.*

~ Shanti Rubenstone ~
Sunday sermon, March 18, 2018

DISCERNING GOD'S WILL

*Dear Divine Ma,
What do You want me to learn today?*

"It's time to stop worrying that others might want to divert your attention from the things you are doing. You need to be doing what you do best. No, even more than that is needed. You need to be doing My will alone. There is nothing worth doing that is outside of My will."

{ How can I ensure that it's Your will that I'm following, and not my own self-will? }

"Raising your attention to Me, and then listening in the heart is your way to know My will."

{ Yes, but that isn't a method that many will access. How can others know Your will? }

"Each must find his or her own way. Some will find Me through My answers to their prayers, some through quiet intuition, some by watching what actually works, and following that."

{ This last way seems like a suspect way to discern Truth. }

"Well, it is not foolproof! But it does lead many, over time, in the right direction. If the universe doesn't support what they are doing, inevitably it won't work in the long run."

{ But, oh, what suffering it brings them in the short run! }

"Yes, yours is a much surer way: talking to Me, asking for My guidance, and listening for My answers in the heart. This is how answered prayer works."

{ But even that, too, has its drawbacks. Many hear what they *want* to hear. It isn't always easy for people to discern true guidance, is it? }

~ MAY 2014 ~

RIGHT ENVIRONMENT FOR FINDING GOD

*Dear Divine Ma,
What do You want me to learn today?*

"It's time to start remembering that in your work, you are growing people more than you are growing products. Their souls are providing the fertilizer, the nutrients that are growing the people you work with daily. They have everything they need within themselves to grow. The only element that is lacking is a supportive environment. If they are surrounded by love, acceptance, devotion, and genuine caring, their souls will have all they need to help them find their way to dharma and to God.

"In a way, doing your dharma and finding Me are one and the same. If you find God's will, that IS God. It is God's will that you realize your Oneness with Him. Find dharma, and you will find Me right around the corner. At Ananda you are blessed to have an environment that is rich in the spiritual ingredients needed to blossom as devotees: encouragement, opportunities for *seva*, time for quiet, and love and devotion. All else—your daily work— is just preparing the soil."

~ MAY 2014 ~

He will whisper to us through our conscience. Look at those things that keep repeating in our mind. That is [the guru] trying to give you your roadmap, to give you your direction ... Our job is to cooperate with grace ... What's the result when we sincerely, authentically try to tune in our consciousness to [the guru's] consciousness? Swami did that throughout his life. In the last few years of his life, he began to say, "I can't tell anymore where Master ends and I begin. It has merged together." There was always [an inner] dialogue going on between him and [his guru].

~ **Nayaswami Jyotish Novak** ~
Inner Renewal Week lecture, Feb. 21, 2018

FOLLOW ME

*Dear Divine Ma,
What do You want me to learn today?*

"Overcome the fear of what others are thinking.
Your job now is to reach out to Me. God alone!*
Go ahead and listen to all of the other inputs,
and smile at them—but follow Me alone!
I am the One, the Only, the source of life and
wisdom and each of your inspired intuitions.
Why would you wish to follow anything but Me?
Does this sound egotistic?
I am merely telling you what is.

"I can show you the path to your own higher Self.
Is there any other goal to which you aspire?
Everything that you do for Ananda and its leaders is
meant to attune you more closely to Me—
to God alone. As Swamiji's wonderful chant says,
'God alone's all we ever need.'† I love you.
I am your center. I am your worth.
I am all-in-all to you."

~ JUNE 2014 ~

* Gyanamata, *God Alone*
† Swami Kriyananda, in his chant "St. Teresa's Admonition"

CHAPTER 8

THE PRESENCE OF GOD

*Strain does not seem to [help].
The moment I feel something
"let go" inside, lo, God is here!
It is a heart-melting "here-ness,"
a lovely whispering of Father
to child, and the reason I did not
have it before, was because I
had failed to let go…
Fellowship with God is like
a delicate little plant.
It vanishes in a second of time,
the very moment, indeed,
one's eye ceases to be "single."*

~ **Frank Laubach** ~
Letters by a Modern Mystic, p. 26

DIVINE MOTHER WAS HERE

*Dear Divine Ma,
What do You want me to learn today?*

{ You were here with me today. You are everything and I am nothing. I opened my heart to You, and You *did* "enter and take charge of my life."* Oh, what thrill upon thrill broke over my consciousness. My heart burst with joy, and the spiritual eye shone as brightly as ever. You came to me as Joy. The divine laughter wanted to cry from my lips, yet I held You locked in my heart. Oh, Divine Mother, *You were here*. You have come to me. Now, when I am finally ready to 'make me the sea'†—when my little wave seemed so unimportant, when surrendering to You was all I craved—now You, Yourself, have come to me. }

"Thou art the sweetness which I do seek...
I taste Thy name; so sweet, so sweet!"‡

~ AUGUST 2004 ~

---

* Swami Kriyananda, Ananda's Purification Ceremony
† Paramhansa Yogananda, *Cosmic Chants,* "I Am the Bubble"
‡ Paramhansa Yogananda, *Cosmic Chants,* "Thou Art My Life"

WHERE ELSE WOULD GOD BE?

*Dear Divine Ma,
What do You want me to learn today?*

{ Help me to sit still, so that I might find the awareness of Your presence. I have waited so long without receiving actual evidence of Your being. I am not complaining, but oh, how I long to have the joy of Your *darshan* again. Swamiji is my polestar. I will be content with whatever You will offer. But I yearn to see Thee, Lord. I love You so much. Help me to awaken from my dream into Thy Light. I love You, Lord. Help me to know You. }

"But I've always been here! Where did *you* go? I am always present. Just 'open your heart to Me, and I will enter and take charge of your life.'"*

{ O Blessed One, You are here! }

"Where else would I be—*could* I be?"

~ OCTOBER 2004 ~

---

* Swami Kriyananda, Ananda's Purification Ceremony

*It's about
emptying out,
so God
can fill
your vessel.*

~ **Nayaswami Jyotish Novak** ~
Inner Renewal Week lecture, Feb. 15, 2018

OPEN YOUR HEART TO THE GURU

*Dear Divine Ma,
What do You want me to learn today?*

"My sole desire for you is that you find your own higher Self. I want nothing else from you but your own highest good. You are blessed to have the great spiritual key of Kriya Yoga, as well as a great guru and teacher. Your guru is the one who can lead you to the Light. Guru is nothing but a guide. You must be thankful for what the guru does on your behalf. Respect and love the guru. 'The guru is your raft over the ocean of delusion.'* Let nothing stand between you and your guru. Let no habit, no old ways of thinking, no unsettling desires keep you from opening your heart to your guru. Be blessed by him. Never belittle him. Always revere him. And know beyond a shadow of a doubt that you are saved only by his intercession. Nothing else is as important as his help."

~ NOVEMBER 2004 ~

* Bhagavan Krishna, Bhagavad Gita

LEARN FROM SWAMIJI

Dear Divine Ma,
What do You want me to learn today?

{ What do you want from me today? }

"Only your love and devotion. These alone do I ask of you. I own the universe, yet I lack only your love. When that is fulfilled, the universe is complete. This is *samadhi*, completion, union. Nothing else is amiss. Yes, the path is long, with who knows how much karma to resolve. But that is as it should be. Your only requirement is this: have you loved God enough? The rest of the world must take care of itself.

"You are greatly blessed to have Swamiji as your guide. Don't let this opportunity pass. This is your chance to find God. Will you let such a priceless opportunity slip away? Why waste time? It might be an entire lifetime before you receive another chance such as this one. You have been given all of the tools you need, right now, to know Me. *Do it now!*"*

~ DECEMBER 2004 ~

* Swami Kriyananda, *Do It NOW!*

*I have done
nothing but
open windows—
God has done
all the rest.*

~ **Frank Laubach** ~
Letters by a Modern Mystic, p. 1

THE SOLUTIONS YOU NEED ARE AWAITING YOUR DISCOVERY

*Dear Divine Ma,
What do You want me to learn today?*

"The magnet that holds the world together is love. If you love enough, all difficulties will be overcome. You imagine that your problems are bigger than you can handle, but they never are. The problem-oriented mind is too complex, but problems never are. Problems invite solutions that simply await your discovery. No obstacles can stand in God's way. This is a blessed time for you! You are fortunate to be living in India, working under Swamiji's guidance. He is one of the great ones dwelling on the earth at this time. It is a great blessing that you are able to serve him as you do. Do not take this time for granted!"

~ DECEMBER 2004 ~

YOU'LL FIND GOD QUICKEST IF YOU DO YOUR GURU'S WILL

*Dear Divine Ma,
What do You want me to learn today?*

"I want you to do My will, and My will is that you do whatever Swami asks. You are blessed to receive and follow his guidance. What he asks will be what I want for you. When he asks you to work in our store, work in his store. It is an honor to work for Swami. Do it—don't hold back. Do what he asks, and you will find Me much more quickly. Don't resist. Do only what he wants, and you will find liberation in this lifetime. It is a blessing. It is an honor to be guided by one so great, so close to Me. Just 'open your heart, and he will enter and take charge of your life.'* What is the difference between Swami and Me? Only a name, and the thinnest veil of joy. Only a veil!"

~ MARCH 2005 ~

---

* Swami Kriyananda, Ananda's Purification Ceremony

My only business now is to persevere in His holy presence. I do so by a simple and loving attention to the Lord. Then I have the experience of the actual presence of God. To use another term, I will call it a secret conversation between my soul and the Lord.

~ **Brother Lawrence** ~
Practicing His Presence, p. 77

WALKING WITH THE GURU

*Dear Divine Ma,
What do You want me to learn today?*

{ I just spent a delightful, even blissful, fifteen minutes walking with my guru. I used my new mantra, and I felt that he was walking beside me, telling me jokes, hugging me, and even tickling me. It was sublime to be able to sustain that feeling so consistently and persistently. I cannot remember another time when I've been able to practice *japa* to such effect— repeating a mantra, over and over. In the past, my mantra was addressed to some impersonal principle, or a far-away God. Today, perhaps for the first time, I directed my mantra to my living guru. And what a difference it made! It was a bit like the powerful result of my prayers twenty years ago when I shifted my praying away from the idea of a distant God, and started talking directly to the Divine Mother. }

~ APRIL 2009 ~

WISDOM IS ONE MANIFESTATION OF GOD

*Dear Divine Ma,
What do You want me to learn today?*

{ What a trip! We just completed a two-hour guided Kriya Yoga meditation. I found myself doing practices from yoga, Islamic Sufism (forearms vertical with palms facing my chest), mystical Christianity (hands folded over the heart), and Raja Yoga (seeing the indigo-violet-blue disk of light after performing *jyoti mudra*). God came in this last form, but also as a powerful shaking energy that comes with spontaneous "davening"—bowing repeatedly as in the Jewish tradition. I am feeling great love in my heart for all, and a deep calmness after overcoming bodily restlessness. The wisdom of these insights is also one of the manifestations of God.
I am peace. I am joy. }

~ JUNE 2009 ~

*I come to tell you all of Him …
To those of you who have asked me
to guide you to my Beloved's silently
talking mind… or whisper to you
through my love. But when I shall
become only… a silently speaking
voice… I will smile in your mind
when you are right, and I will whisper
to you through your conscience,
and I will love through your love …
As soon as you know my Beloved and
hear His voice in silence, you will
know me again more tangibly than
you knew me in this earth plane.
And yet when I am only a
dream to you… we all will be
ever awake in Him.*

~ **Paramhansa Yogananda** ~
from the poem *When I Am Only a Dream,* Inner Culture, 1940

GOD WAS THERE

*Dear Divine Ma,
What do You want me to learn today?*

{ The sound of AUM was there, booming like a mighty waterfall. The light at the spiritual eye was there, shining in the darkness, bathing me with its Light. "Out of the darkness, out of the silence, Thundered the Cosmic Sound, Amen!"* How else do I know that God has come? By the internal voice of true Wisdom. By the bliss that I felt when I heard the gong sound over and over while walking at the Meditation Retreat. By the power and energy that gives strength and perseverance when others are saying, "It can't be done!" By the peace I feel when sitting in *sadhana*, looking at Paramhansa Yogananda's photo. By the chuckling, bemused calmness that comes over me when the village crazy man is yelling abuses and lifting his walking stick threateningly. By the love that I feel for Swamiji when reciting my *japa*. }

~ AUGUST 2009 ~

* Swami Kriyananda, Ananda's Festival of Light

SEE THE GOLDEN RING

*Dear Divine Ma,
What do You want me to learn today?*

"It's time to realize that we aren't meditating to earn a gold star on some wall chart, but to see the golden ring and white star in the forehead. Only the inner star is worth seeing, and this is why we meditate. Continue with your efforts to dive deeply and see the star, and to hear its vehicle, its carrying energy, the sound of AUM. Light and sound are two aspects of AUM—they are manifestations of God in a form that you can perceive. If you can see the Light, or hear the rumbling of AUM, sounding like the soft rumble of electrons whirling around their atom, then you *have* 'seen God,' as the Bible promises. Yes, people can 'see God.' But only those who are willing to draw the Divine Presence by uplifting their consciousness to Him."

{ So, we do the "heavy lifting." Then it will feel like God's grace has descended to us. But *we* are the ones doing the moving. }

"God never moves, nor is ever more available than right now."

{ It is we who must do the changing! }

~ MAY 2011 ~

God speaks
with our voices,
if we respond
to His every
whisper.

~ Frank Laubach ~
Practicing His Presence, p. 33

PUT ALL YOUR ENERGY INTO IT

*Dear Divine Ma,
What do You want me to learn today?*

"You have to put *all* of your energy into anything you really want. Isn't this a quality you are known for? Yet when it comes to God you are strangely passive in the face of failure. Why do you accept failure? You behave as if you don't actually believe it's possible to know God. If you don't, then why continue the charade? Whom are you trying to impress?"

{ No one, Lord. It's true that I often don't actually expect God to come in my meditations. But Swamiji said that we should meditate, and that's good enough for me. Do I believe that God is reachable? Hmm, perhaps by some. But by me? I've meditated for twenty-nine years, and I *have* had glimpses of Her—in the form of light, as a tunnel, as sounds, and as an inner shaking. But She never stays longer than a minute or two, often less. And it sometimes seems a fruitless endeavor to perceive Her so rarely, and then only for a few moments. Is that all there is? The great Western mystic Frank Laubach knew God much more intimately. He is a good model for me. }

"Don't *want* to see Her. *Talk* to Her."*

~ MAY 2011 ~

* Frank Laubach, *Letters by a Modern Mystic*

EGO SPEAKS THROUGH THE VOICE – THE HEART SPEAKS IN SILENCE

*Dear Divine Ma,
What do You want me to learn today?*

"Relate to Swami as your own higher Self. Be respectful. Be non-attached. Be unselfish. Give him his privacy. Let him know that you adore him, but don't make a big show of it. Let him feel your heart, and hear less of your voice. The ego speaks through the voice, but the heart speaks in silence. Want only what he wants. Want nothing from him, only that he might receive what he needs and wishes. Remember that you serve 'at his pleasure.' You tend to do things that you imagine he wants. But let him decide."

~ MAY 2011 ~

This is the best way to act: talk a great deal [with] the Lord. . . . Oh, if we only let God have His full chance He will break our hearts with the glory of His revelation... *It is [my] business to look into the very face of God until [I] ache with bliss.*

~ **Frank Laubach** ~
Letters By a Modern Mystic, pp. 66–67

SO MUCH BLISS THAT NOTHING ELSE MATTERS

Dear Divine Ma,
What do You want me to learn today?

{ I want to understand Your play. But of course that probably is not possible, is it? }

"To understand is either to know all, or to be in so much bliss that nothing else matters."

{ Well, I can never know it all like You, because *You* are omniscient. But perhaps I can be in so much bliss that the details will no longer matter. And then, if one brother misunderstands and blames me, it will just be part of Your cosmic joke. I do take it all so seriously, don't I? Yet You *chuckle* at it all, don't You? Why can't I chuckle when others 'revile me for righteousness' sake?'* }

"Consciousness is everything. All else is chaff."

~ NOVEMBER 2011 ~

---

* Jesus, the New Testament

GOD WAS HAPPENING TO ME

*Dear Divine Ma,
What do You want me to learn today?*

{ As I sat in meditation before tonight's New Year's Eve ceremony, both the sound of AUM and the light at the spiritual eye came as clearly as ever. I was drawn into breathlessness without any effort on my part. I was clearly not the cause. God "was happening" to me. During the Purification Ceremony that followed, it was utterly clear that God was the Doer—that it wasn't anything we ministers were doing that was blessing those people. During the Purification Ceremony and the Festival of Light, Swamiji's presence comes as a powerful flow of divine energy. Swamiji, you have given us so much. I am humbled by the Power that appears as if from nowhere and flows through me. I don't ask for it. It comes unbidden. I reckon It knows when I need Its help. }

~ JANUARY 2013 ~

To rouse God ... unceasingly offer deep, inward mental-whisper prayer demands... Thus, a new awakening will come, a new living relation with God will be established. The mist of silence and mystery, which hangs over everything, will slowly vanish before the dawning light of your mental whispers for God ... Listen!

Through thy soul-stirring whispers He is whispering songs of His love unto thee everywhere. When your unceasing whispers shall at last dig deep into the soil of Omnipresent Silence, the fountains of His answering whispers will gush forth from your soul and with their life-giving waters refresh thirsting hearts everywhere.

~ **Paramhansa Yogananda** ~
The original *Yogoda Lessons* 1930, Super-Advanced Course, 2-5

BLISS IS THE GOAL

*Dear Divine Ma,
What do You want me to learn today?*

{ Oh, it was good to feel You so clearly in nature and the trees today. The trees and I were One. You are the Presence that binds us together. I am blessed to have received You so clearly, so tangibly. I love it when Your presence is so clearly with me. But then, if it were obvious to everyone, all the time, would it be as special as it is now? }

"Yes, that's what Satya Yuga—the highest of the four ages through which this planet cycles—is like. No one ever tires of true bliss. No one wants duality. Everyone wants union, except that the wise don't just talk about it—they act on it consciously, deliberately. The true goal of life is Bliss. When we awake spiritually, it seems so natural, as if we had never forgotten that bliss, and then we begin to act in ways that will attract that bliss to us again and again. Simple!"

~ MARCH 2013 ~

Afterword

MY LOST MUSIC SPRANG FROM THE HEART OF EVERYTHING

Paramhansa Yogananda, *Whispers from Eternity*, p. 151

I heard sweet, enchanted music playing faintly beneath the sounds of my outer life, as if coming from forgotten dreams. Still-ly I listened, and the music grew more and more subtle, poignant, and sweet, drawing me inward until I could hear it no longer with my earthly ears.

Patiently I waited, striving to think whether I'd ever heard earthly music like the divine nuances of these new melodies. No. In my rich storehouse of memory I found no likeness to those enchanting sounds that had come and gone in my consciousness, like phantoms of idle reflection.

Had I really heard that music, or had I only imagined its sweet harmony? Was it the exquisite expression of my subtle, highest aspiration, or was it only the sound of harmonious whispers of passing fancy?

I waited. Deeply, inwardly, I listened . . . Suddenly, in deepest silence, those ancient sounds returned, swelling up from beneath hidden memories of my soul . . . I needed no other sounds, no other vibrations of earthly fulfillment to satisfy my heart.

Then it was that the lost music of my soul resounded at the heart of everything, pulsing from the very heart of all my private dreams . . .

> *Behind the curtains of life's ceaseless play,*
> *I found again,*
> *Playing on harp strings of all deep feeling,*
> *The lost, but now found,*
> *Beloved music of my soul!*

GLOSSARY

Sources

- **AN** *Letter*, by Asha Nayaswami
- **AY** *Autobiography of a Yogi*, Paramhansa Yogananda
- **EBG** *The Essence of the Bhagavad Gita, Explained by Paramhansa Yogananda, As Remembered by His Disciple*, Swami Kriyananda
- **GTA** *God Talks with Arjuna*, Paramahansa Yogananda
- **HTM** *How to Meditate*, Jyotish Novak
- **LIM** *Lessons in Meditation*, Jyotish Novak
- **RO** *A Renunciate Order for the New Age*, Swami Kriyananda
- **RY** *The Art and Science of Raja Yoga*, Swami Kriyananda
- **SKL** *Swami Kriyananda: Lightbearer*, Asha Nayaswami
- **TP** *The New Path: One Man's Quest On the Only Path There Is*, Swami Kriyananda
- **WE** *Whispers from Eternity*, Paramhansa Yogananda, Edited by his direct disciple, Swami Kriyananda

---

agya vs. ajna | Sanskrit words that are generally written with a "jn" but pronounced with a slightly nasal "gy" are treated more phonetically in Ananda books. In 1950, Yogananda told Kriyananda, " 'jn' is how scholars usually write it. I can't see why. It isn't pronounced" that way. [EBG]

ananda | Sanskrit for "divine bliss"; a worldwide movement based on the teachings of Paramhansa Yogananda and founded by Swami Kriyananda, a direct disciple of Yogananda. [Ananda.org]

ashram | A place of retirement from worldly life for the purpose of pursuing spiritual practices. [TP p. 134]

AUM (or Om) | The vibrational sound of the cosmos. [EBG] The vibration of the Cosmic Motor. AUM the blissful Comforter is heard in meditation and reveals to the devotee the ultimate Truth. [AY p. 145] invisible life force which divinely upholds all creation. AUM can be heard by a Self-realization technique of meditation. "Amin" is used by the Moslems, "Amen" by the Christians, "Hum" by the Tibetans, and "AUM" by Hindus. [WE]

avidya | Individual delusion that clouds man's perception and gives him a false concept of reality, giving him the illusion of having his own separate reality [GTA p. 80], which creates ego-consciousness. [GTA p. 11]

Babaji | Guru of Lahiri Mahasaya [AY p. 292] a deathless avatar still living secretly in the Himalayas His powers are Christlike. [WE]

bhav | One's particular spiritual approach, manner, mood, style, atmosphere, or feeling.

Biraj | Spiritual name bestowed on the author by Swami Kriyananda in 2008. Swamiji said the name means: "Having a presence" or "Knowing one's Self."

Brahma (*pronounced bram-ha*) | The all-pervading Spirit as the originator of all creation. [WE] The Supreme Spirit, God.

darshan | The blessing which flows from the mere sight of a saint. [AY p. 165]

davening | More correctly known as shuckling, is the ritual swaying of worshippers during Jewish prayer, usually forward and back but also from side to side, to increase concentration and emotional intensity. [Wikipedia]

dharma | Doing those divinely appointed actions that will take you toward increasing inner freedom. Duty as inherent in the circumstances in which a man finds himself. Virtue, righteousness, right action. [EBG]

energization | A set of 39 exercises developed in 1916 by Yogananda specifically to teach how to gain greater control over the flow of *prana*, or life-force, in the body. (LIM, ch. 5)

energizing | To conduct the spiritual practice of the energization exercises, or to supply energy or vitality to some part of the body.

Festival of Light | Written in 1986, it put Ananda's central message into a ceremony that could be repeated week after week, so the impact of the Sunday Service wouldn't depend so completely on the speaking ability of the minister. [SKL]

guru | The word guru is often applied, broadly, to any venerated teacher. On the spiritual path, however, it refers to the sadguru or true teacher: that enlightened sage who has been commissioned by God to lead the spiritually fit seeker out of darkness, and into the experience of Supreme Truth. [TP p. 134] Spiritual savior. [EBG]

Hong-Sau | Two sacred Sanskrit chant words possessing a vibratory connection with the incoming and outgoing breath.... literally, "I am He." [AY, pp. 383–84] A Self-Realization technique of meditation.

japa | The constant repetition of God's name. [EBG]

jyoti mudra | A technique taught to Kriya Yogis for the purpose of manifesting the light (jyoti) of the spiritual eye found in the forehead.

karma | Effects of past actions, in this or a former life; from Sanskrit kri, "to do." [AY p. 35] The natural principle of cause and effect. [AY p. 231] The karmic law requires that every human wish find ultimate fulfillment. Desire is thus the chain which binds man to the reincarnational wheel. [AY p. 302] The cosmic law of cause and effect: "as you sow, so shall you reap."

Kauravas | The 100 sons of Dhritarashtra in the Indian epic, the *Mahabharata,* and the war with their cousins, the Pandavas, in the war of Kurukshetra.

Kriya | See Kriya Yoga.

Kriyananda | A direct disciple of Paramhansa Yogananda since 1948, he was the founder, spiritual guide, and creative force behind Ananda. The liturgy, scripture commentary, and most of the music you hear at Ananda were written by him. During his life, he wrote nearly 150 books and nearly 400 pieces of music. He divided his time between Ananda residential communities in India, Europe, and America. [SKL]

Kriya Yoga | A yogic technique whereby the sensory tumult is stilled, permitting man to achieve an ever-increasing identity with cosmic consciousness. [AY p. 9]] The ancient yogic science reintroduced to the world by Lahiri Mahasaya in the nineteenth century. It consists of the careful, conscious circulation of energy around the spine in order to magnetize it and to redirect the mental tendencies toward the brain. [EBG]

mantra | Potent vibratory chant. The literal translation of Sanskrit mantra is "instrument of thought," signifying the ideal, inaudible sounds which represent one aspect of creation. [AY p. 453]

master | We call Yogananda "Master" in the sense of teacher. He is a true master of the practices in which we ourselves are struggling to excel. [TP pp. 245–46]

maya | Delusion. [EBG] Cosmic delusion. The function of maya is to attempt to divert man from Spirit to matter, from reality to unreality. [AY]

Nayaswami Order | a reformation of the ancient swami order. This new order is of "nayaswamis." "Naya" means "new," to indicate the new spirit for Dwapara Yuga. The old order, founded in Kali Yuga, the Age of Matter, had to be concerned with the form of things, with many rules about what a swami could and could not do. The Nayaswami Order is defined more by consciousness. [AN, letter from Assisi, Italy 11/21/09] The old method of renunciation was world-negating; the new one is samadhi-affirming. One's concentration, in other words, is on the joy of soul-freedom in God. [RO Chapter 5]

nirbikalpa samadhi | *Nirbikalpa samadhi* is unconditioned ecstasy: one's consciousness has become so established in oneness with God that there is no possibility of a return to the limitations of the ego. [EBG]

Pandavas | The sons of Pandu in the Indian epic, the Mahabharata, and the war with their cousins, the Kauravas, in the war of Kurukshetra.

Patanjali | Compiler of the *Yoga Sutras*, one of the most important texts in the Hindu tradition and the foundation of classical Yoga. He lived somewhere between 200 BC and 200 AD.

prana | The vitalizing power, or life-force (variously called prana, chi, or ki), that surrounds as well as flows in all living forms, and the energy that flows up in the subtle spine in conjunction with inhalation, and down with exhalation. [HTM p. 38]

Purification Ceremony | An Ananda ceremony that affirms outwardly, as well as inwardly, an attitude of self-offering to the divine.

sabikalpa samadhi | *Sabikalpa samadhi* is conditional ecstasy. There is still a possibility of return to the limitations of the ego. [EBG]

sadhana | Path of spiritual discipline; path or preliminary road to God. [AY pp. 20, 85] Spiritual practice. [EBG]

samadhi | Divine ecstasy. Such cosmic consciousness is the state of infinite awareness that comes to the yogi once the hypnosis of ego has been broken. Christian saints have sometimes described this state as "mystical marriage," for in it the soul merges into God and becomes one with Him. [TP p. 196] Literally, "to direct together." Samadhi is a superconscious state of ecstasy in which the yogi perceives the identity of so soul and Spirit. [AY p. 107]

samskaras | Subtle tendencies; "seeds" of karma; the result of repeated actions (karmas) of the past—not only of this life, but of many past incarnations. Each samskar constitutes a subtle vortex of energy. [RY p. 400] A thought or act once performed does not cease to be, but remains in the consciousness as an impression, tendency, or urge that influences us to repeat those thoughts or actions until they become habits. [GTA p. 49]

sangha | Association (of truth-seekers). Fellowship with others of shared spiritual aspiration. [WE]

satchidananda | Ever-existing, ever-conscious, ever-new Bliss. [EBG]

Satya Yuga | A 4800-year period [7,700–12,500 AD] when the intelligence of man will be completely developed; he will work in harmony with the divine plan. [AY p. 167] The golden age of wisdom. [EBG p. 175]

self | The egoic part of one's being, as opposed to the Soul that is that part that is a reflection of God within us.

Self | Soul: Individualized Spirit, which is unmanifested, ever-existing, ever-conscious, ever-new Bliss. The soul, as Spirit's reflection, has the same qualities as Spirit. The soul's subjective consciousness in connection with the body and its relations is termed the "ego," or the "pseudo-soul." [Paramhansa Yogananda, Inner Culture magazine, Sept. 1939] The long bridge over the chasm between ego-consciousness and God-consciousness. [RY p. 393]

seva | Service thinking only of God, or selfless service conducted as much as possible without being attached to the fruits of your labors.

swami | One who has achieved mastery of him or her self. Sanskrit root meaning of swami is "he who is one with his Self (Swa)." Applied to a member of the Indian order of monks, the title has the formal respect of "the reverend." [AY p. 17] He renounces all egoic identification with the world, and considers himself belonging to the entire human family. [WE] Swami is the title commonly given to sannyasis (renunciates), in affirmation of the truth that he alone is a true ruler in this world who is the ruler of himself. [TP p. 135] In this book, "Swami" almost always refers specifically to my own spiritual teacher, Swami Kriyananda (1926–2013).

Swamiji | Ji is a customary respectful suffix, particularly used in direct address; thus, "swamiji," "guruji," "Sri Yukteswarji," "paramhansaji." [AY p. 86]

tapasya | Austerity, in the sense of renunciation as a joyful self-offering to God. [SKL p. 333] Spiritual disciple and self sacrifice. Very demanding work with many obstacles to overcome.

Vishwarupa | In chapter 11 of the Bhagavad Gita, Krishna reveals himself as the Supreme Being, where the whole universe is contained in him, by displaying this Vishwarupa to Arjuna, who experiences it with divine vision endowed to him by Krishna. A related vision of Krishna's Vishwarupa was witnessed by Krishna's mother Yasoda when he was a toddler.

Wayne | The given name of the author before receiving from Swami Kriyananda in 2008 the spiritual name of Biraj.

yuga | Ages or cycles of time; the four ages are Kali (dark), Dwapara ("second," an age of energy), Treta ("third," an age of awareness of the power of mind), and Satya ("Truth," also called Krita, an age of high spiritual awareness) yugas. [EBG

BIBLIOGRAPHY

Abell, Arthur. *Talks With Great Composers.* New York: Citadel Press, 1994.
à Kempis, Thomas. "That We Should Disdain Vain Secular Learning." *The Imitation of Christ.* New York: Doubleday Image, 1989.
Asha Nayaswami. Sunday sermon at Ananda Palo Alto, Feb. 14, 2016.
Asha Nayaswami aka Asha Praver. *Swami Kriyananda As We Have Known Him.* Nevada City: Crystal Clarity Publishers, 2006.
Asha Nayaswami. *Swami Kriyananda: Lightbearer, The Life and Legacy of a Disciple of Paramhansa Yogananda.* Palo Alto: Chela Publications, 2019.
Byasa, Beda. Kriyananda (ed). The Bhagavad Gita. Nevada City: Crystal Clarity Publishers, 2008.
Gupta, Mahendranath, *The Gospel of Sri Ramakrishna: According to M.* Madras: Sri Ramakrishna Math, 1942.
Gyanamata, Sri. *God Alone: The Life and Letters of a Saint.* Los Angeles: Self-Realization Fellowship, 1984.
Jesus Christ, The New Testament, NIV. Grand Rapids: Vondervan, 2015.
Kriyananda, Swami. "About Spiritual Marriage." A talk given January 1981.
Kriyananda, Swami. *Art as a Hidden Message: A Guide to Self-Realization.* Nevada City: Crystal Clarity Publishers, 1997.
Kriyananda, Swami. *The Art of Supportive Leadership.* Nevada City: Crystal Clarity Publishers, 1987.
Kriyananda, Swami. *Awaken to Superconsciousness.* Nevada City: Crystal Clarity Publishers, 2008.
Kriyananda, Swami. *Cities of Light.* Nevada City: Crystal Clarity Publishers, 2004.
Kriyananda, Swami. *Conversations with Yogananda.* Nevada City: Crystal Clarity Publishers, 2003.
Kriyananda, Swami. *The Essence of Self-Realization.* Nevada City: Crystal Clarity Publishers, 1990.
Kriyananda, Swami. *A Handbook on Discipleship.* Nevada City: Crystal Clarity Publishers, 2010.
Kriyananda, Swami. *The Hindu Way of Awakening.* Nevada City: Crystal Clarity Publishers, 1998.

Kriyananda, Swami. "How Should We Relate to You, Swami?", in *In Divine Friendship*. Nevada City: Crystal Clarity Publishers, 2008.

Kriyananda, Swami. *Intuition for Starters*. Nevada City: Crystal Clarity, 2002.

Kriyananda, Swami. *The Land of Golden Sunshine: An Allegory of Soul-Yearning*. Nevada City: Crystal Clarity Publishers, 2002.

Kriyananda, Swami. *Meditation for Starters*. Nevada City: Crystal Clarity Publishers, 2008.

Kriyananda, Swami. *"Music, Creativity, and Superconscious Experience."* A talk given June 19, 1996.

Kriyananda, Swami. *The New Path*, Nevada City: Crystal Clarity Publishers, 2009.

Kriyananda, Swami. *Rays of the One Light*. Nevada City: Crystal Clarity Publishers, 1996.

Kriyananda, Swami. *Revelations of Christ: Proclaimed by Paramhansa Yogananda*. Nevada City: Crystal Clarity Publishers, 2007.

Kriyananda, Swami. *The Rubaiyat of Omar Khayyam Explained*. Nevada City: Crystal Clarity Publishers, 1994.

Kriyananda, Swami. Sunday sermon at Ananda Palo Alto, March 5, 2000.

Laubach, Frank. *Letters by a Modern Mystic*. Colorado Springs: Purposeful Design, 2007.

Lawrence, Brother and Laubach, Frank. *Practicing His Presence*. Beaumont: Seed-Sowers, 1973.

Novak, Nayaswami Jyotish. *How to Meditate*. Nevada City: Crystal Clarity Publishers, 2008.

Novak, Nayaswami Jyotish. Inner Renewal Week lecture at Ananda Village, Feb. 15, 2018.

Novak, Nayaswami Jyotish. Inner Renewal Week lecture at Ananda Village, Feb. 21, 2018.

Rubenstone, Shanti. Sunday sermon at Ananda Palo Alto, March 18, 2018.

Russell, A.J. *God Calling*. Uhrichsville: Barbour, 2011.

Yogananda, Paramhansa. *Autobiography of a Yogi*. Nevada City: Crystal Clarity Publishers, 1995.

Yogananda, Paramhansa. *God Talks with Arjuna: The Bhagavad Gita, Royal Science of God-Realization*. Los Angeles: Self-Realization Fellowship, 1995.

Yogananda, Paramhansa. *How to Be Happy All the Time*. Nevada City: Crystal Clarity Publishers, 2006.

Yogananda, Paramhansa. *How to Have Courage, Calmness, and Confidence*, Nevada City: Crystal Clarity Publishers, 2010.

Yogananda, Paramhansa. The original *Yogoda Lessons*. 1925.

Yogananda, Paramhansa. The original *Yogoda Lessons: Super-Advanced Course*. 1930.

Yogananda, Paramhansa. *Whispers from Eternity: A Book of Answered Prayers*. Nevada City: Crystal Clarity Publishers, 2008.

About the Author

BIRAJ WAYNE PALMER

Biraj Wayne Palmer has been meditating for over 35 years, since becoming a disciple of Paramhansa Yogananda in 1983.

Biraj has served the Ananda organization on two continents, and in more than a dozen capacities: educator, dairyman, carpenter, book salesman, retreat leader, teaching center manager, store manager, construction supervisor, choir director, discussion leader, lecturer, organic farmer, and chant leader.

He is the author of one other book, *The Intuitive Gardener: The Man Behind Ananda's Meditation Retreat Garden*, Santa Cruz: Blue Bone Books, 2019.

He shares a home with his wife Nayaswami Lahari Elizabeth, in the Palo Alto, California, Ananda Community.

Spiritual Guides

PARAMHANSA YOGANANDA

"As a bright light shining in the midst of darkness, so was Yogananda's presence in this world. Such a great soul comes on earth only rarely, when there is a real need among men."
—The Shankaracharya of Kanchipuram

Born in India in 1893, Paramhansa Yogananda was trained from his early years to bring India's ancient science of Self-realization to the West. In 1920 he moved to the United States to begin what was to develop into a worldwide work touching millions of lives. Americans were hungry for India's spiritual teachings, and for the liberating techniques of yoga.

In 1946 he published what has become a spiritual classic and one of the best-loved books of the twentieth century, *Autobiography of a Yogi*. In addition, Yogananda established headquarters for a worldwide work, wrote a number of books and study courses, gave lectures to thousands in most major cities across the United States, wrote music and poetry, and trained disciples. He was invited to the White House by Calvin Coolidge, and he initiated Mahatma Gandhi into Kriya Yoga, his most advanced meditation technique.

Yogananda's message to the West highlighted the unity of all religions, and the importance of love for God combined with scientific techniques of meditation.

SWAMI KRIYANANDA

"Swami Kriyananda is a man of wisdom and compassion in action, truly one of the leading lights in the spiritual world today."

—Lama Surya Das, Dzogchen Center, author of *Awakening the Buddha Within*

A prolific author and composer, and a world-renowned spiritual teacher, **Swami Kriyananda** (1926–2013) referred to himself simply as a humble disciple of the great God-realized master, Paramhansa Yogananda. During a period of intense inward reflection, he discovered Yogananda's *Autobiography of a Yogi* at the age of twenty-two, and immediately traveled three thousand miles to meet the Master, who accepted him as a monastic disciple. Kriyananda served him during the last four years of the Master's life, and dedicated the rest of his life to sharing Yogananda's teachings throughout the world.

Yogananda appointed him as the head of the monastery, authorized him to teach in his name and to give initiation into Kriya Yoga, and entrusted him with the missions of writing and developing what he called "world brotherhood colonies."

Recognized as the "father of the spiritual communities movement," Swami Kriyananda founded Ananda World Brotherhood Community in the Sierra Nevada foothills of Northern California in 1968. It has served as a model for eight communities founded subsequently in the United States, Europe, and India.

ANANDA SANGHA WORLDWIDE

Ananda Sangha is a fellowship of kindred souls following the teachings of Paramhansa Yogananda. The Sangha embraces the search for higher consciousness through the practice of meditation, and through the ideal of service to others in their quest for Self-realization. Approximately ten thousand spiritual seekers are affiliated with Ananda Sangha throughout the world.

Founded in 1968 by Swami Kriyananda, a direct disciple of Paramhansa Yogananda, Ananda includes seven communities in the United States, Europe, and in India. Worldwide, about one thousand devotees live in these spiritual communities, which are based on Yogananda's ideals of "plain living and high thinking."

Swami Kriyananda lived with his guru during the last four years of the Master's life, and continued to serve his organization for another ten years, bringing the teachings of Kriya Yoga and Self-realization to audiences in the United States, Europe, Australia, and, from 1958–1962, India. In 1968, together with a small group of close friends and students, he founded the first "world-brotherhood community" in the foothills of the Sierra Nevada Mountains in northeastern California. Initially a meditation retreat center located on sixty-seven acres of forested land, Ananda World-Brotherhood Community today encompasses one thousand acres where about 250 people live a dynamic, fulfilling life based on the principles and practices of spiritual, mental, and physical development, cooperation, respect, and divine friendship.

At this printing, after fifty years of existence, Ananda is one of the most successful networks of intentional communities in the world. Urban communities have been developed in Palo Alto and Sacramento, California; Portland, Oregon; and Seattle, Washington. In Europe, near Assisi, Italy, a spiritual retreat and community was established in 1983, where today nearly one hundred residents from eight countries live. And in India, devotees are coming together in rapidly increasing numbers to share this life and these teachings amongst themselves and with others.

THE EXPANDING LIGHT

The Expanding Light Retreat, a nonprofit organization, offers many public retreat programs—spiritual growth retreats, spiritual travels, yoga trainings—based on the universal teachings of Paramhansa Yogananda, the world-renowned author of *Autobiography of a Yogi*. Our retreat center is situated within the 1,000 beautiful acres of Ananda Village, just outside Nevada City, California.

Guests have visited here for almost 50 years, from all parts of the world, with many different spiritual perspectives, to learn more about the path of Kriya Yoga meditation, Ananda Yoga for physical and spiritual healing, and the contemporary application of Yogananda's teachings to help people realize their true potential.

Founded by Swami Kriyananda in 1969, Ananda Village is a spiritual cooperative community, an expression of one of Paramhansa Yogananda's ideals that people live together harmoniously, united in the goal of Self-realization. Ananda Worldwide has communities on the West Coast, and in Europe and Asia.

Ananda's primary goal is to help people achieve Self-realization: a state of consciousness that comes through shedding all outward self-definitions. Ananda has, therefore, created communities and centers that welcome all sincere seekers, regardless of race, religion, national origin, gender, sexual orientation, age, or disability. We are committed to providing an inclusive, welcoming environment for everyone to pursue the search for God.

Guests at The Expanding Light can learn the four practices that comprise Yogananda's teachings of Kriya Yoga: the Energization Exercises, the *Hong-Sau* technique of concentration, the AUM technique, and Kriya Yoga. The first two techniques are available for all guests; the second two are available to those interested in pursuing this path more deeply.

Blue Bone Books
Santa Cruz, CA

Blue Bone Books publishes poetry, children's and spiritual books that have relevance to today's cultural changes necessary to inspire our new emerging world culture. There are three divisions:

Spiritual Books

We are interested in publishing books that make a difference. Love makes a difference. Our spiritual books support self love, Self love and rites that bring people together.

Poetry

We publish multi-genre poets who are also painters, photographers, book artists, singers, and seers. The books showcase their talents with their original visual or musical work presented with the poetry.

Children's Books

We are now introducing books that respond to parents' growing demand for spiritually uplifting reading materials. Our books help children develop Self-esteem, featuring values-driven stories for all ages.

SPIRITUAL BOOKS

Heart Path
Learning to Love Yourself and Listening to Your Guides
Robin White Turtle Lysne, M.F.A., Ph.D.

A book for everyone interested in understanding how self love leads to Self Love. In fact, learning to love the self is the essential link standing between us and spirit. Full of guided imagery inspired by the author's guidance,

Heart Path is a process based on the Bodhichitta form of Tibetan Buddhist meditation. However, the meditation as experienced in *Heart Path* supports a recognition of the various aspects within a person that need the love of our higher and wiser selves. Dr. Lysne outlines five aspects that are essential in a whole person, and gives the reader ways to become more aware of them within the self.

The book also gives the reader the ways to connect with their divine guidance. Based on classes taught by the author over a six year period, the book reveals answers to metaphysical questions answered by Dr. Lysne's Guides and transcribed by the author to support each person's healing and growth. *Heart Path* is a book for anyone wanting to grow and know their Divine Source more thoroughly.

Path of the Heart CD
Robin White Turtle Lysne, M.F.A., Ph.D.

This CD helps you find the path to your heart. It also helps you connect with your spiritual guides and angels. Offering you guidance and free-choice in creating your sacred space, a safe and nurturing place within, this CD is relaxing and healing as you listen to it. Use as a means to heal your heart's desire. The CD is professionally recorded, approximately 45 minutes in length with music by harpist Adam Free.

Heart Path Handbook
An Energy Medicine Guide for Therapists and Healers
Robin White Turtle Lysne, M.F.A., Ph.D.

This handbook offers the reader ways to love themselves without limits. It teaches Therapists and Healers how to use Heart Path, a process the author teaches in workshops and seminars. Details include illustrations of how people present various configurations in their energy fields, such as getting "twisted around themselves," or aligning with their light as well as illustrations of the aura, chakras, and how we function metaphysically. A treasure for anyone interested in letting go of "victim/perpetrator" and other negative patterns, with lessons, guided imagery, and support through its workbook format.

You Long for Me
A Devotional Offering to the Divine Presence in Each of Us
Amità

A poetic reflection on Divine Nature. It gives the reader pages to reflect on, offering time to breathe and to feel one's true nature. An essential bedside reader. Amità holds a direct transmission to the Awakened State. All one needs to do is to surrender and sit in her presence.

Ceremonies from the Heart
For Children, Adults and the Earth
Robin White Turtle Lysne, M.F.A., Ph.D.

Bring more meaning to life's transformative moments with these initiation rites and ceremonies, offered by true practitioners. Meant to inspire, there are rites for adolescents, moving in, moving out, menses and sexuality, and for boys and men, as well as various phases of our lives through menopause, illness, and death. The last section supports rites for the Earth, the Great Healer, who needs our help at this critical time.

POETRY BOOKS

Poems for the Lost Deer
Robin White Turtle Lysne, M.F.A., Ph.D.

This book of poems is at once a testament, a praise, and a lament for Nature and what we are doing to our Mother Earth. The news articles and interviews of an actual event in 2008 document the poems. Native Wisdom in harmony with nature is contrasted with Western-based capitalism. The book addresses women's issues, emigration, and what patriarchy assumes it can do in our own National Park Service.

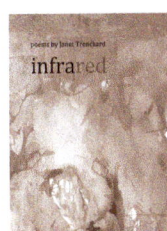

Infrared
Janet Trenchard

Trenchard pairs her artist's keen eye with equal attention to language's music and rhythm to create an at times haunting collection where goddesses and gods walk among us, mere mortals rise from ashes, and where that which falls apart finds shape and meaning once more. Unforgettable. —*Sally Ashton, Santa Clara County Poet Laureate*

Understory
Marcia Adams

The kind of inspired poet who takes us exploring. As she grows up in Northern California, discovers WWII history in a collection of love letters, wades through sorrow, and dives into joy, we delight and laugh along with her. I treasure her words. You won't want to miss this lovely writer. —*Linda Helding, Explorer*

Visible Light
Stuart Presley

Stuart Presley's work is subtle, funny, and ironic, with a twist of the extraordinary. Always in his work, both in his photographs, and poems, a nod to what is out there to ponder and to the cosmos.

"Between the world as it is, and isn't, Stuart Presley finds the luminous difference."
—*Michael Hannon, Poet, author of 35 poetry titles*

Mosaic
Robin White Turtle Lysne, M.F.A., Ph.D.

A book of tenderness, awe, and depth. Lysne explores the natural world in the manner of the mystic. With a keen eye and open heart, she communes with wolf, owl, raven, and cat. Her poems reach deeply into relationships between family members, friends, and lovers. Throughout this vast collection, Lysne's brave poems explore the joys of a life richly lived and challenge us to do the same. —*David Denny, author of* Some Divine Commotion

The author invites you also to explore these titles:

Autobiography of a Yogi
Paramhansa Yogananda

One of the best-selling Eastern philosophy titles of all time, with millions of copies sold, this book was named one of the best and most influential books of the twentieth century. This highly prized reprinting of the original 1946 edition is the only one available free from textual changes made after Yogananda's death.

How to Awaken Your True Potential
The Wisdom of Yogananda Series, Volume 7
Paramhansa Yogananda

Are you ready to take serious steps to discover the hidden resources of divine joy, love, and power within you? In this book you'll find step-by-step guidance to help you discover that hidden within you is untold power, and you will learn how to take steps daily to live life with greater joy and meaning.

Whispers from Eternity
Paramhansa Yogananda
Edited by His Disciple, Swami Kriyananda

Many poetic works can inspire, but few, like this one, have the power to change your life. These verses rank with the greatest mystical poetry of all time: the works of St. John of the Cross, Rumi, Kabir, Mirabai, and Omar Khayyam. In this book Paramhansa Yogananda—the great master of yoga and author of the classic *Autobiography of a Yogi*—shares his exquisitely beautiful thoughts and words filled with longing for the Divine. Yogananda was not only a spiritual master, but a master poet, whose poems reveal the hidden divine presence behind even everyday things.

Each of these prayer-poems has been spiritualized by this great man of God. Open this book, pick a poem at random, and read it. Mentally repeat whatever phrase appeals to you. Within a short time you will see your consciousness transformed. This book has the power to rapidly accelerate your spiritual growth, and provides hundreds of delightful ways for you to begin your own conversation with God.

Intuition for Starters
How to Know and Trust Your Inner Guidance
Swami Kriyananda

More than just a "feeling" or a guess, true intuition is one of the most important—yet often least developed—of our human faculties. This book straightforwardly explains what true intuition is, where it comes from, and the attitudes necessary for developing it, and gives you easy-to-understand practices and guidelines that will help you tap into intuitive guidance at will.

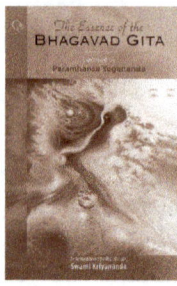

The Essence of the Bhagavad Gita
Explained by Paramhansa Yogananda
As Remembered by His Disciple, Swami Kriyananda

Rarely in a lifetime does a new spiritual classic appear that has the power to change people's lives and transform future generations. This is such a book. This revelation of India's best-loved scripture approaches it from a fresh perspective, showing its deep allegorical meaning and its down-to-earth practicality. The themes presented are universal: how to achieve victory in life in union with the Divine; how to prepare for life's "final exam," death, and what happens afterward; and how to triumph over all pain and suffering. Swami Kriyananda declared, "Yogananda's insights into the Gita are the most amazing, thrilling, and helpful of any I have ever read."

Swami Kriyananda, LIGHTBEARER
The Life and Legacy of a Disciple of Paramhansa Yogananda
Asha Nayaswami

In the early 1970s, Swami Kriyananda asked a young student named Asha to start taking notes for the book he knew she would someday write. He explained himself to her in a way he did to only a few others. Since then, she was in constant contact with him, as a devotee, friend, personal assistant, and eventually, a spiritual teacher in her own right.

Swami's life was a triumphant life, but not an easy one. Plagued by ill health, financial challenges, and years of bitter estrangement from fellow disciples, his life story is told in the struggle as well as the victory. This firsthand account is more than a biography. It's a guidebook for spiritual living, a path of light that all may follow.